Praise for *Ins*

"A tremendous resource, amalgamating commentary from ... that is presented in a concise, easy to read format." – Alan H. Aronson, Shareholder, Akerman Senterfitt

"Aspatore's *Inside the Minds* series allows strategic professionals to access cutting-edge information from proven experts in the field. Their approach of providing consolidated, valuable, current information reflects their true understanding of the life of an executive. We need the best information in the most concise format. Aspatore is a consistently reliable resource that provides great information without expending unnecessary time." – Kimberly L. Giangrande, Principal, Intuitive HR

"A terrific compilation of real world, successful strategies and practical advice." – Sig Anderman, CEO, Ellie Mae Inc.

"Must read source for leaders wanting to stay ahead of emerging best practices and to understand the thought processes leading up to the innovation." – Mark Gasta, SVP and Chief Human Resources Officer, Vail Resorts Management Company

"A refreshing collection of strategic insights, not dreary commonplaces, from some of the best of the profession." – Roger J. Magnuson, Partner, Dorsey & Whitney LLP

"Unique and insightful perspectives. Great to read and an excellent way to stay in touch. – Filippo Passerini, President of Global Business Services and CIO, The Procter & Gamble Company

"A must read for C-level and senior executives. The information is based on actual experiences from successful senior leaders and has real, practical value presented in a very useable format." – Stephen Fugale, VP and CIO, Villanova University

"Some of the best insight around from sources in the know" – Donald R. Kirk, Shareholder, Fowler White Boggs PA

"Powerful insight from people who practice every day!" – Andrea R. Bortner, VP, GCSD Human Resources, Harris Corporation

"Aspatore's *Inside the Minds* series provides practical, cutting edge advice from those with insight into the real world challenges that confront businesses in the global economy." – Michael Bednarek, Partner, Shearman & Sterling LLP

"Outstanding insights from respected business leaders." – R. Scot Sellers, CEO, Archstone

ASPATORE

Aspatore Books, a Thomson Reuters business, exclusively publishes C-Level executives and partners from the world's most respected companies and law firms. Each publication provides professionals of all levels with proven business and legal intelligence from industry insiders—direct and unfiltered insight from those who know it best. Aspatore Books is committed to publishing an innovative line of business and legal titles that lay forth principles and offer insights that can have a direct financial impact on the reader's business objectives.

Each chapter in the *Inside the Minds* series offers thought leadership and expert analysis on an industry, profession, or topic, providing a future-oriented perspective and proven strategies for success. Each author has been selected based on their experience and C-Level standing within the business and legal communities. *Inside the Minds* was conceived to give a first-hand look into the leading minds of top business executives and lawyers worldwide, presenting an unprecedented collection of views on various industries and professions.

Creating an Effective Marketing Message

Leading Marketing Executives on Developing Communication Strategies That Articulate the Brand and Resonate with Target Audiences

ASPATORE

For additional copies or customer service inquiries, please e-mail west.customer.service@thomson.com.

ISBN 978-0-314-28682-6

Mat #41386976

CONTENTS

How to Use Data to Drive the Creation of Your Marketing Message

Gregory Marcus Bibas
Chief Marketing Officer
3 Day Blinds

ASPATORE

Introduction

I joined 3 Day Blinds (a private equity-owned portfolio company owned by TPG Group) in December 2010 as the senior vice president of marketing and part of a new management team designed to revitalize our business. In April 2012, I was promoted to the chief marketing officer role. My prior background is in direct marketing, as well as management consulting, with some more focused direct marketing consulting for fifteen years. My current role is focused on these objectives:

- Brand stewardship and defining the value proposition conveyed, brand style, key messages, and consumer experience
- Go-to-market strategy that boils the company value proposition down into the key ideas and conveys it across every customer touch point within the organization
- High return on marketing investment (ROMI) lead acquisition, which is converted into scheduled in-home appointments for our design consultants
- Tools for our design consultants to generate their own appointments through relationships and referrals
- Company growth strategy, partnerships, and innovation

Company Growth and Change

The company was at an inflection point, having shifted from an in-store retail strategy to an in-home sales model supported by what was then an anemic lead-generation and appointment-setting operation. The challenge was rapid growth in appointments, leading to rapid growth in sales.

On my first day with the company, we conducted a messaging workshop that pulled together consumer research that had previously been done with the feedback and input of customer service, front-line sales, and the marketing consultants who had been managing the marketing of the business prior to my arrival. Of key importance here was to ensure that we not only got the best ideas out on the table, but also began to create a consistent message as to the value proposition the company offered to achieve buy-in, so that all parts of the business could speak the same language and feel they had a part in creating the messaging the company would use. Marketing cannot live in an ivory tower and create on its own; it must function as an integral part of the organization and achieve buy-in with other teams.

Primary Challenges

The first real challenge I faced was in educating the company on what it meant to create a data-driven marketing organization and implement the data-capture and reporting capabilities required to make informed choices about the success of individual marketing initiatives, which focused on different messages for different audiences. Three months in, with the beginnings of a marketing team hired and a rudimentary set of data tracking, we began testing our marketing messages.

Appropriate Use of Consumer Research

While an internal messaging workshop and consumer research are good first steps toward figuring out what the company value proposition should be and provides the first rough draft for how to craft an effective marketing message, experience has taught me that what consumers say is important and what they respond to in practice are two different things. This is why it was important for us to build the capability to track accurately the data associated with individual marketing campaigns. Which ones provided the highest volume? The lowest-cost lead? The highest conversion from lead to booked appointment? Appointment to sale? Highest sale value? All of these variables play into the profit equation of our business.

Determining Company Variables

Since not all businesses are driven by the same variables, defining that profit equation for your specific business and then ensuring that each of the critical value drivers is captured in your marketing metrics will allow you to determine which different messages might drive more leads, which tactics drive more conversion, and which drive more purchase spend. Aligning the best of each of these variables from the various tests you have conducted into combinations, which are also tested, starts to produce exponential growth of ROMI. Obviously, defining each test clearly and trying to test variables in mutually exclusive ways to isolate which individual part of the message is driving results, is critical.

Company Values within the Marketing Message

The values our company competes on are speed, personalized service, and trust. Initially, these values were not as clearly defined in our messaging, as we tested which approaches consumers responded to best for our brand. It is important to realize that the marketing messages you focus on should be both differentiators with your competitors and values your company can actually deliver so that there is alignment between what you are promising in your marketing messaging and what all the various parts of your organization can deliver in the consumer experience. If the messaging is differentiated, but the experience is not, or that experience is not aligned with the promise in the messaging, you have a recipe for failure.

The development of those messages came from building a mental picture of our customers in profile form from the previously completed consumer research. We used appended data on customers who had purchased from us to determine what our customers looked like and what they liked to buy, as well as how much money they made, and built a mental image of how we believe they lived their lives. Before picking which message we would test, we used the developed consumer image and guessed at how that type of customer might want to consume our service or product, thereby determining how they would likely respond to different messages. We also figured out where those types of customers would be most accessible to us in our marketing efforts and began to develop sources to test.

Differentiating the Message and the Brand

To determine how we should differentiate our message and our brand, we look at the marketplace and try to define what each of our competitors focuses on as its value and key selling points. While we may not be exactly right about their focus, each company conveys its key selling points to its customers, so it becomes obvious which areas it is competing in, when paying attention to competitor marketing material. We focus on speed, personalized service, and trust. Companies are constructed differently with different structural advantages, so more often than not these key selling points, or unique selling propositions (USPs), are different. Where they are not, the difference comes down to how those values are lived and executed.

When your competitors focus on price or style and fashion, and you focus on speed and personalized service, you need to make sure you stay true to what your company values are in your promotions and ensure that your front-line sales team knows how to address sales objections without compromising your values. It is more difficult for the low-cost provider to compete with personalized service, and more difficult for the personalized service provider to compete with low cost. Both strategies will find customers who hold their key value as important, and some customers who find both important must choose which is more important to them. Having a strong communication of commitment to those key values, which is shown to the customer through the alignment of the organization's delivery with its expectation creation, then becomes the differentiator, which creates trust and brings the customer to the point of purchase.

Implementation of Values

If your value is speed, it means from the first customer call, you must deliver speed. You must answer your phones quickly, schedule an appointment quickly, and offer quick shipping and installation options. If you under-deliver on the customer's expectations, you must work quickly to resolve those mistakes because even with high service levels, there will be dissatisfied customers. Play out what you believe your customer will expect of you based on the picture of your customer that you have developed and what you know about how they respond to different marketing and promotional messages.

Objective Metrics of Success

Each of the points of service delivery (or customer interaction around those core brand values) can be measured so that there are objective metrics of success and failure internally in your organization on which you can improve through focus and alignment of the organization. This measurement is important to the evolution of the marketing message and the success of marketing campaigns in helping define which words, images, and offers you use in your promotion. While the measurement of these metrics is typically managed by customer service, creating a tight feedback loop to share data and learning from what is heard on the phones and in conversations with customers among marketing, customer service, and sales is critical to guiding that message evolution in the right direction.

Evolution of Company Messaging

While those values of speed, personalized service, and trust are core concepts we use in our messaging, the words used to describe them to our customers were tested in multiple iterations of direct mail, e-mail, search engine marketing campaigns, telemarketing, etc. The company's messaging and value propositions are constantly evolving in response to the customer's responsiveness to specific marketing campaigns. The dynamic evolution of the company's messaging is driven by actual responsiveness to promotions and revenue generated. If you have defined your core customers well, your message will not swing wildly as it changes, but will evolve over time to the best version of your message and value proposition, getting tighter with each iteration, as you focus on the core components your customers respond to, engage with, and ultimately value.

If you have disparate groups of customers who value different parts of what you offer, the same process holds true, but has to have two or more parallel iterative processes running and testing to achieve the best version of messaging for each group, as if each were a completely separate customer base and completely separate product or service offering. This process will also make more obvious those areas where additional development and focus within the organization are required. If your customers value something your company is not delivering or not delivering well, this iterative testing and feedback loop process will reveal the shortfall more rapidly and help quantify the likely size of the opportunity.

Data Usage in Marketing

The approach I have described here is based on direct marketing philosophy, and is strongly data-driven, but it extends backwards into the organization to help the organization evolve based on consumer demands and response to messaging about differentiators offered by the company. This means that it relies on a close partnership with information technology (IT) to implement the data-gathering systems and respond to frequent requests for custom reporting, as well as working with finance to set up reporting and analysis to constantly evaluate different aspects of the marketing initiatives being launched and where the financial return is strongest on a heatmap of the various marketing tests developed.

This approach is difficult to implement without trust and a track record of success within an organization. Building up the early successes from the initial direct marketing tests we launched gave me the organizational buy-in and "permission" to broaden the scope of marketing's mandate, and begin to integrate more tightly how multiple functions interact with the customer.

Alignment of Marketing Messaging

After a year of this iterative process of testing, analyzing, refining, and testing some more, we went back and took another look at the original messaging workshop, revising our value propositions to bring them into alignment with what we were delivering and what our customers were responding to. We did a re-launch of our go-to-market messaging, aligning what our marketing messaging says with what our call center agents tell our customers, what our design consultants tell our clients at an appointment, all the way through to installation and service.

When a customer sees a promise and then experiences it in practice, that alignment increases service scores as expectations are being fulfilled. Our customer satisfaction survey results now show 90 percent satisfaction due to the alignment between messaging and delivery our team achieved. This is not a result driven by marketing, but by the combined efforts of marketing creating an expectation that is then delivered on by customer service, sales, manufacturing, and installation services in an aligned way.

Implications for Business Growth

The implications for the growth of the business have been substantial and sustained. During the first six months in the role, as we built the foundation of this iterative system, appointment growth was flat. Since then, year-over-year (YOY) growth each month has been 20 percent to 30 percent, which flows through to increased sales. As we approach the one-year anniversary of this initial uptick, we continue to see opportunity to grow and expect to lap our growth with continued 20 percent to 30 percent YOY growth.

Conclusion: Key Components of Marketing Message Success

There is no simple marketing message success formula to apply to every business because each one is different, but the process of discovery and development we have used to create and optimize our marketing message can be applied to disparate businesses:

1. Gain alignment on the best rough draft of what the key differentiators are that the business has to offer.
2. Achieve clarity on your company's profit equation, and identify the variables you need to track in your marketing and sales process to determine which marketing messages and initiatives are driving results.
3. Implement a good data-tracking system to record, compare, and analyze the results of your various tests.
4. Use research and your current customer base to help create a picture or pictures of your ideal buyers; hypothesize about how those consumers would consume your product or service; and test different messages surrounding those hypotheses.
5. Determine which important values that customers hold are in alignment with what your company can deliver well, and focus on those messages, while also trying to better deliver some of the other things your customers value (assuming they are consistent with distinct customer groups you are targeting).
6. Create a tight feedback loop with customer service, sales, and anyone else on the front line with consumers to get additional data on what is important to your customers.
7. Measure, analyze, iterate.

Key Takeaways

- Marketing must function as an integral part of the organization and achieve buy-in with other teams to create successful marketing strategies.

- A company's marketing message must both differentiate from your competitors' messages and align with the service and product you can actually deliver.
- All employees, from sales to installation, must be aware of company values to ensure promotions and messaging stay true to the company values on all levels of customer interaction.

Gregory Marcus Bibas is currently the chief marketing officer for 3 Day Blinds, a private equity-owned vertically integrated manufacturer of window treatments, where he is responsible for growing the marketing funnel, increasing the efficiency of marketing capital, defining and communicating the brand message, defining growth strategy, innovating, and developing tools to help customers and the company's 200-plus design consultants to improve their ability to serve customers.

Prior to his role at 3 Day Blinds, Mr. Bibas was a management consultant with Bain & Co. in New York, where he helped his clients across multiple industries and capabilities. Before his work at Bain & Co., Mr. Bibas spent fifteen years as both an operator and a consultant in direct marketing-oriented operations, business development, and marketing roles, helping companies large and small to grow their customer bases and revenues.

Mr. Bibas holds an MBA in finance and strategy from the Wharton School of Business and a BA in philosophy from the University of Pennsylvania.

New Media and the Importance of Message Strategy

Mary Anne Keegan

Chief Marketing Officer

BillGuard

ASPATORE

Introduction

Marketing as a profession has seen many changes in recent years, but many of the fundamental practices for message development still apply: no matter what else changes, marketing must be clear, concise, and created with an understanding of the audience. However, today's customers are no longer happy to sit back and receive messages passively. Instead, they want to participate actively in the conversation, to share ideas, and in many cases to receive something of value from the company in exchange for their thoughts and insights. The customer has moved to the front line of publishing information on a company's product, service, or brand.

Today's buyers spend more time conducting online research than ever before. They rely on their social channels, both offline and online, to gather information, gain buy-in, and make purchasing decisions. That is why it is so vital to provide your prospects with information that addresses their concerns and encourages them to take the next step in the sales cycle.

Social media, like Twitter, Facebook, Google+, and many others, have dramatically changed the channels marketers can leverage to deliver their message. As a result, marketers have had to learn how best to manage and deliver their messages using these new channels. Never before has the need for a company message strategy been more important.

The message strategy is the foundation for all marketing activities and includes not only verbal messages, but also nonverbal elements, like imagery, corporate color palette, corporate font family, and key words and phrases. A clear message strategy ensures that all company materials and communications are written in a consistent style and makes it easier to deliver the same message across all marketing media—web, sales collaterals, social channels, investor decks, public relations, and advertisements.

It is also important that your message be delivered with one voice, from the receptionist all the way to the company executives. The more times prospects and customers hear the same message repeated, the more likely they are to remember it and ask to learn more.

Developing Effective Marketing Messages

Once the company message strategy is defined, you can begin developing *marketing messages* about your product, service, or company. These messages will explain to your audience how they should think about your brand. When developing an effective marketing message, some key elements to consider include:

1. *Define the overall objective and purpose of the message.* What problem are you trying to solve and what action do you want to result from the message?
2. *Have a solid understanding of the customer.* What is the persona of your customer-type—needs, behavior, interests, content consumption styles? The better you understand your customer, the better you will be able to define the information to share, how to say it, and how to deliver it.
3. *Create relevant content, and in the case of social marketing, make it personal.* What is in it for your audience? Think about this from the customers' perspective—not yours. Remember that people buy benefits, not product features. Irrelevant content can lengthen the decision-making process by almost 20 percent. In the case of business-to-business (B2B) marketing, content must revolve around subject matter expertise. Your focus should be, "How can we help you?" not "How can we *sell* you?"
4. *Be authentic.* Regardless of the audience, messaging needs to be genuine. It has to be credible, real, and defensible.

Content Marketing, Thought Leadership, and Communication Strategies

New technology has created a fundamental shift in the way our audiences consume information. As a result, it is important that marketers invest in new strategies that connect with their prospects and customers in more personal ways. One of these strategies is *content marketing,* sometimes referred to as *thought leadership marketing.* In essence, content marketing is the art of creating and sharing value-based information that attracts and engages a specific audience to either build loyalty with, or consume, your brand. Good content marketing can help companies achieve a variety of business goals, including generating sales leads, educating and/or entertaining audiences, increasing brand awareness, and supporting customer retention. Because it is a "push" strategy, it attracts a more qualified lead base.

We are bombarded with thousands of messages every day, so it is no surprise that the best way to connect with your target market is to publish information that makes your audience stop and react in a desired way. Content marketing can make that happen over a wide range of media. Some of the channels content marketing touches include:

1. Blogs and microblogs
2. Case studies
3. White papers
4. E-newsletters
5. Mobile apps
6. "How-To" articles
7. Infographics
8. Social media posts
9. Videos
10. Webinars/webcasts
11. Events
12. Gamification

A fairly new format for sharing your messaging is through "gamification"—turning your message into an interactive game. Marketers are beginning to use gaming as a new medium for distributing key product messaging. Properly executed, games can be an effective framework for sharing and teaching your audience about your brand and product in a fun and engaging way. After all, who doesn't like a good game?

Making the Most of Your Content

Good content can and should be re-purposed so you do not have to write new content every day, which can become quite expensive for smaller companies and a drain on resources. For example, content from a webinar can be summarized into a how-to article and then summarized inside an e-newsletter that links back to the full article.

In addition, by adding an element of "social sharing" to your content, you can foster a peer-referral element that will also extend the lifecycle of the content you develop. This creates a viral behavior that allows your users to spread your message for you—the more cross-over the better, especially when you consider that content does not necessarily get consumed the day it is published. In fact, studies show that people need to see your message at least six times before they trust you. Developing content with a longer shelf life and being patient are important considerations when focusing on content marketing. It takes time to build credibility.

Content Curation

A complementary strategy—one that is fairly new to content marketing—is *content curation*—the practice of finding content relevant for your target market and sharing portions of it (e.g., on a blog), while crediting the original source and linking to it. Not only does this build your company as a thought leader in your industry, but it also helps your audience navigate the clutter of information on the Internet by having you act as a content aggregator on a specific type of content.

An easy way to get started is to begin curating recent news in your industry, along with relevant videos and pictures. Additionally, if you write articles and link to other key posts on other sites, this will show your audience other perspectives on a similar topic. Tools you can use to help curate content include Twitter Lists, Google Reader, Google Alerts, and Paper.li:

- Using your *Twitter* account, you can create a list of people who share good content and from whom you glean good information to share with others.
- *Google Reader,* like other Rich Site Summary (RSS) readers, allows you to collect, track, and select articles of relevance.
- *Google Alert* presents you with articles that mention a pre-selected term. This helps pre-filter content to find the most interesting pieces.
- *Paper.li* is a free online tool that lets you create your own virtual newspaper by pulling content from the links of the people you follow on your Twitter and Facebook accounts.

But how do you create good and relevant content? One common practice is to tell a good story. Think of a good book you recently read. You were probably hooked by some content that drew you in and made you want to read more. In essence, the author made a connection with you through the content he or she wrote. It is the same with good content marketing—if you select information that is relevant and of value to your audience, they are more likely to be interested and tune in to the messaging.

Essentials for Creating Engaging Messaging

People remember much more about your company or product when it is shared with them in the form of a story. A message that is personal, engaging, and sometimes funny helps tell a good story and shape perceptions about your brand and make it memorable. Stories help us understand new concepts better than dry facts and figures. As with any story, it is important that your message create an experience for your target audience. Do not just tell them: use graphics; encourage interaction; and draw the audience in by having them scroll and click through.

When developing your marketing story you should:

1. *Focus on the emotions customers will seek out and enjoy in your brand or product.* What is on the mind of your audience that you can either *help with* or *connect on?* Understand their problems, issues, needs, and wants. For example, if you sell shoes to women with large feet, your audience may be upset with not being able to find large sizes in shoes. Use that emotion when telling your story.
2. *Be descriptive and use good images.* Provide as much detail as possible so that they can visualize what you are communicating.
3. *Be engaging.* Make the content interactive where it makes sense. This allows your audience to self-select where they want to go next, or be directed to different content based on how they are interacting with you. This allows the user to gain more value and allows you to educate them more effectively.
4. *Be real.* Avoid being so effusive that you begin to lose credibility. Be authentic and trustworthy.
5. *Keep it simple.* The story should be understandable to a child. Use simple language and short sentences.

6. *Inject an element of surprise.* Everyone loves a story that introduces the unexpected or has an element of amazement.

But what happens if someone *else* tells a story about your company or brand? With the rise of social media, the audience sometimes has more control over your brand identity than you do. Bad reviews are far more viral than praise. When this happens, you have only one option—deliver a solution that goes above and beyond what is expected. Your effort will be shared via social channels and will soon become the new story.

Starting the Conversation

Social media do not change the message—they simply speed its delivery and broaden its distribution. Social media do, however, change the tone of the discourse. Social networks are platforms for personal conversations and connections, so they require a more conversational tone when speaking with your audience. Companies need to develop new brand voices to stay engaged in this conversation.

Keeping your voice consistent across channels, however, can be more difficult than it may appear. For example, because of its 140-character limitation, Twitter mimics conversational patterns that exist between friends in online and offline environments more closely than Facebook. Facebook requires more in-depth information because of the sheer volume of posts that have to be moderated. Nevertheless, companies need to make sure that all content stays true to the brand's voice and the company's purpose, even across vastly different channels.

When using social channels to spread your message, be generous. Social media are all about conversation, content, and engagement. It is a "give-to-get" model. You must give information freely to get users to connect and come back for more. Being generous with your content will help shape your brand message and will make users want to sign up or follow. In return, over time, you will receive insights into your target audience.

It is important to have someone check social media outlets daily and provide, when appropriate, answers to questions and comments on communication threads on your brand. Keep in mind that how you respond may be the first insight a future customer has to your company. Never be confrontational. Make every experience with your brand amazing.

Conclusion

Through your content, you develop attention, then interest, then action. Demonstrating expertise and insight in your domain and sharing that knowledge freely is important when trying to connect with new prospects in the digital age.

As the marketing profession continues to evolve and social channels take center stage, one reality is coming into focus: brands are becoming more visual. You can see this occurring all around us with new social networks like Pinterest and recent enhancements like Facebook Timeline. What this means for marketers is that brands need to have strong visual elements that include strong imagery, solid visual vocabulary, and an eye for visual storytelling that helps paint a picture of your message across social channels. As the old saying goes, "A picture is worth a thousand words," or perhaps today, "A visual brand is worth a million impressions."

Key Takeaways

- Today, the customer has become the front line for spreading your brand message, which makes the company's message strategy more important than ever. The message strategy is the underpinning of all marking activities, encompassing verbal messages, imagery, colors, and tone.
- The message strategy is the foundation for developing your marketing messages. Keep your messages grounded in your overall brand purpose, your understanding of customer problems, and authenticity.
- Content marketing and content curation both offer a path through the digital noise to your target audience. Both strategies position the company as a thought leader and a source of meaningful, engaging expertise for the customer.
- Share your messages in the form of stories to make them more personal and engaging. When you interact on social media, be generous and open. Today's marketing is all about conversation.

As chief marketing officer for BillGuard, a personal finance security company, Mary Anne Keegan oversees the development and execution of the company's marketing and corporate communication strategies, protecting consumers from unfair and unauthorized charges on their bills. BillGuard was recently inducted into Online Banking Report's Hall of Fame as one of the top online banking innovations of all time, and has been featured prominently in the Wall Street Journal, New York Times, *and* The Economist, *as well as on ABC and CBS News. Mary Anne joined the company after spending six years at Early Warning Services, a leader in fraud prevention solutions, where she was chief marketing and sales officer. During her tenure she launched the Early Warning brand and received more than thirty national and global awards for marketing and media production. As a contribution to the industry, she developed an annual summit to push forward the importance of data collaboration to protect the financial eco-system from fraud.*

Ms. Keegan also held executive marketing positions at First Data, the world's largest provider of merchant processing services, and at Primary Payment Systems, a financial services start-up where she was involved in expanding the company from 20 to over 200 employees, and contributing to its sizable financial growth and acquisition.

A Message in Motion: Creating a Messaging Foundation That Moves Across Markets, Audiences, and Delivery Platforms

Theresa Damato

Vice President, Marketing

Trustwave Inc.

ASPATORE

Introduction

In my marketing roles over the years, I have worked to define corporate identity, creative, branding and positioning strategies, as well as develop new positioning and messaging for emerging solution areas, create marketing and communications approaches for new markets and geographies, and establish unique value propositions for individual products and services. My charter on any given day at Trustwave can range from determining how our brand is to be represented in creative, to where it will be seen, to how it will flow internally and externally across multiple communications vehicles for customers, prospects, and employees around the world.

In the technology space, the pace is fast, and portfolios are always rapidly evolving to stay in front of market demands and the ways customers buy. In this industry, we often have to create new messaging and value propositions to map to evolving business outcomes, combine products and solutions into one cohesive use case, and align products in a more unified manner to communicate effectively and focus on adapting to business value. This transformative exercise helps keep the message resonating because we are constantly looking at creating impact with new markets, new audiences, and new stakeholders in ways that matter.

Regardless of whether you are developing a new message or evolving an existing message, it is critical that your organization is able to answer who you are as an organization, what makes your company, solution, or product useful, and how you want to be perceived by your market stakeholders and influencers. It is not enough simply to know the answer to what differentiates the company or the product from a competitive perspective. You are more than someone else's competition. When it comes to your message, your organization needs to know how to answer the questions, *"Who are we, and what do we deliver?"* and be able to answer based on who is doing the asking. Depending on whom you are speaking with, you will need to highlight different strengths or values to align with what is important to your audience. And in some cases, you will need to consider the manner in which you communicate from platform to platform.

Good messaging, in my perspective, can find and articulate that one truth. It identifies the core of who you are, and then it can effectively adapt to changing situations. The goal of this chapter is to help you create a strong foundation for messaging; understand how to measure its impact, and provide considerations for how and when to "convert" your message to achieve the greatest impact, no matter what the platform.

Who Are You? Crafting an Effective Message

It's a Team Effort

The marketing teams are the professionals who take the lead and drive the messaging exercise. They are experienced in and tasked with understanding what makes an impactful message, how it will be communicated, and the right process and contributing stakeholders required to build a message effectively. Outside of the marketing team, other stakeholders who may need to be included in the process are typically executive management, members of the sales force, the customer service team, product management, business partners, customers, and other valuable third-party perspectives, including journalists and industry analysts, for example. This virtual team constitutes the sphere of influence around the message and the brand and works together to contribute to the process. If your company is international, then all messaging exercises should involve global representation because something that plays well in the "home base" may make little to no sense in other local markets.

Balance Emotion with Science

One of the challenges with branding and messaging is that they can be perceived as highly subjective and even emotional. Because these activities are often looked at as nothing more than "creative expression," one of the mistakes organizations make when developing a message is that they can be too casual about the process.

Messaging and branding are persuasive processes. The best practices for developing messaging or positioning start with taking the emotion out and adding much more science. The best outcomes I have seen come from an honest, pragmatic, and almost "uncreative" process because—and this is important—we have to ensure that we know exactly how people feel about our company and our products internally, externally, and competitively, and then develop an effective core for our message based on that. Our brand statements and our messages serve as beacons that drive the company's mission and our strategy for continued growth, from marketing and communications plans to sales conversations to product development and more.

Make sure your messaging process takes a practical 360° view. Gather data; measure responses; consolidate and roll up feedback into foundational tenets; and then add the "creative juice" at the end. A traditional "message map" tool can help keep you on track and ensure that your message and all key points are effectively documented for various groups to use in ongoing activities and conversations.

Is This Thing On? How to Measure Impact

When we want to know how impactful our message is in the market or with key audiences, there are several things we can measure. The three main areas for measuring the impact of marketing and message are usually found in the categories of *awareness, consideration*, and *preference*. Brand *awareness* generally measures our "share of voice" in the market when compared to that of the competition. A close companion to *awareness* is usually brand sentiment, which measures how people feel about our brand. In other words, when it comes to awareness, does our audience know us? Are they talking about us, and if so, what are they saying? Is their feeling about our brand positive, neutral, or negative?

Beyond *awareness*, marketers should evaluate their brand and message performance in the categories of *consideration* and *preference*, which is usually demonstrated by increased prospect engagement with the brand and increased lead-to-revenue ratios. Metrics for this category typically include engagement with content assets, website traffic trends (new visitors, returning visitors), branded Web search volume, top-of-the-lead-funnel activity, improved lead conversions (lead quality), sales pipeline activity, and new and returning customers. The sales team is an excellent resource for gaining field insight around the *consideration* and *preference* categories.

Tracking your brand and specific activities related to key messages can help you measure the impact of your work.

Marketing teams can measure awareness, consideration, and preference in several ways. Many agencies do market studies that can benchmark and track these metrics, and many automated tools are available to track them in-house on demand. In addition, marketers can gather solid, detailed information by using simple instruments like annual surveys of customers and partners or by requesting feedback from market influencers like analysts or journalists.

There is another equally important consideration for measuring the effectiveness of a message, which goes beyond *awareness, consideration,* and *preference* of external stakeholders. One of the key indicators of an effective brand and message can be found right within your own organization. Marketers should ensure that during a brand or messaging initiative, internal employees are engaged, feel positively about the value the company delivers to the market, and are able to articulate the message.

You Are Invited: The Marriage of Medium and Message

The technical process for developing messages has not changed drastically over the years, but the platforms, the vehicles, and the ways we push messages out are dramatically different. In my view, the playing field for communicating a message has become fairly even, no matter who you are. Where it used to be that large companies with big budgets could make the most noise and get the most coverage and attention, this is not necessarily the case today. Online platforms have brought us a lower cost of entry for advertising, as well as the advent of social media, which today gives us access to blogging, online communities, and simpler ways to engage our target audiences immediately.

However, that easy access introduces the requirement for even more discipline regarding your brand and your message. The integrity and context of the message itself and the need for tight, impactful communications are more important than ever. Why? Because platforms that make it easy to push out messages are also responsible for creating a crowded arena and a huge amount of noise in the market. There are also so many more places to get information quickly, which gives your buyer a nearly unlimited amount of data, but within a much shorter attention span.

Just think about yourself for a second—the volume of returns you get in a Web search, the number of pop-up ads you need to navigate, and the number of e-mails, text messages, and instant messages you receive in a single day as compared to five years ago. Making a message stand out is critical, as is delivering a message that is customized and appropriate for the medium— whether that message is crafted as an intriguing, succinct, value-driven online ad campaign, an actionable, instructional piece suitable for a thought leadership blog, or as part of a two-way conversation in a social community.

Welcome to the Future: A Word on Social Media

In business-to-business (B2B) marketing, we are finding that social media are truly changing the ways our messages are being sent and received. Social media force marketers to look at something that may be a bit new to them—two-way conversations with their audience. Social media require us to concede that we cannot drive or control conversations about our brand, and, often, our messages are not being delivered directly by us, but rather through others' conversations about our products or their experiences with our company.

We are still evolving our approach to social media to contribute value effectively and consistently to conversations in our space. One of the simplest ways marketing teams can get started is through a blog. Our organization uses blogs as a way to contribute valuable content, perspectives, and thought leadership. It helps us provide messages and information to our readers quickly, and we can respond rapidly to topics our audience cares about. In that way, it also helps us supplement traditional media relation strategies.

We have also been developing our company's social presence on Facebook and LinkedIn, and on Twitter, we have established a Twitter TweetChat, a hosted forum for discussing relevant topics in our industry each week. During these regularly scheduled sessions, we invite partners, customers, internal teams, journalists, analysts, et al., to discuss issues they are facing and solutions, tips, and tricks. One of our groups has just launched a social media project focused on a specific value proposition for a particular business area. On the platform, customers, partners, analysts, bloggers, and more deliver regular "video keynotes" on various topics; we have an embedded Twitter feed; and our company conducts polls and publishes tips and advice, and we are also running a video contest to further engagement.

In addition to being another means of reaching a potential audience, the insight that can be gained from social media is invaluable. I believe it provides an important perspective for marketers, and it is an effective way to engage in conversations, gauge brand awareness, test messages, and identify trends, and, ultimately, it can even inform product development and help us position our solutions and our brand more effectively.

Conclusion

The core element of successfully creating an effective marketing message is to understand that it is a persuasive process, so make sure your messaging exercise starts with a foundational process. You cannot just sit around a table casually and come up with an effective message. Instead, you have to start with the framework that will inform your brand promise, your unique position, your character and the feelings you want to convey, what point of view you want to share, and additionally, a framework that considers what instruments you will use to get the message across.

Then tap into a broad team for data collection and collaboration, including internal and external stakeholders. Gather and synthesize that input, which will start to inform your core message. From there, it is also important to think about the message from all angles. How will it play out to the audiences who will receive it? How do you adjust your core message for greatest impact with your customers, employees, and partners? What about the general market who has never heard of you? Once you select the messages and the vehicles, test and measure different versions in the market, and track their impact on awareness, consideration, and preference. This allows you to make sure your brand and your messages are effective, and you can demonstrate that you are getting your value across successfully.

And remember, marketing can often get stuck operating in a fish bowl, so check in with your stakeholders frequently. Sales teams, customers, partners, and market influencers are usually more than happy to provide you with real-time, honest input about how your message is resonating, so you can continue to improve, refine, and deliver impactful communications for your organization.

Key Takeaways

- Messaging is not an exact science, but neither is it without science. Treat it like a persuasive process because that is the basis of message development.
- Always include research, testing, surveys, and data analytics in your message strategy, and involve a wide variety of stakeholders in your process to ensure you get a 360° view.
- Without knowing whom you are marketing to, what you are marketing will not matter. Take care to tailor your message depending on who your audience is and what is important to them.
- Know how and where your message will be best delivered, and make sure it fits where you put it. That social media have created the option does not mean the option is the right one for your company.
- Always measure. Collect data; analyze it; and be able to demonstrate the impact of your branding and messaging efforts. *No matter what.*

Theresa Damato is a visionary and passionate marketing leader with nearly twenty years of experience in international technology marketing and communications. She is known for developing and executing brand strategies, creating innovative, high-performing marketing programs, expanding go-to-market strategies, analyzing new markets, and creating new revenue opportunities through both direct and indirect sales models. Her focus is on aligning marketing with revenue and growth strategies and optimizing the impact of marketing on the business and the brand.

Ms. Damato currently holds the position of vice president, marketing at Trustwave, where she is responsible for managing and evangelizing brand identity, reputation, and positioning for the organization. Prior to her current role, she has held marketing leadership positions for some of the world's largest global technology organizations, as well as technology startups. She has managed functions including corporate marketing and communications, product marketing, regional field marketing, and channel marketing for leading technology organizations that include SafeNet Inc., Deutsche Telekom/T-Systems, Aladdin Knowledge Systems, El Camino Resources Ltd., and S3 Networks.

Dedication: *I would like to dedicate this chapter to my mother, Dr. Lois Maschio, who has been encouraging me to express myself through writing ever since I could hold a crayon. She inspires me to seek knowledge relentlessly, and never stop improving the way I communicate my thoughts and ideas.*

Marketing Financial Products to "Main Street" Families

Duane M. Morrow

Chief Marketing Officer,
Primerica Life and Canada Marketing

Primerica

ASPATORE

Introduction

My role in Primerica is to provide the training, products, sales material, and sales tools our representatives need to be able to show up at Main Street tables and deliver for the consumer.

Recent Marketing Initiatives

Our most recent marketing initiative was a rollout for a cutting-edge, unique life-insurance product called TermNOW, which allows us to accept 90 percent of life applications electronically through the web. This feature enables us to sit with a client in their home, and eight out of ten times, we can provide them with a solution at their own kitchen table in less than two minutes via the web. The client even has the ability to except the policy electronically through our client portal, MyPrimerica.com.

Currently, 60 percent of our policies are being delivered electronically. Now that we are able to distribute life insurance rapidly to the consumer and shift to a paperless model, we are better equipped to issue the policy quickly and pay our agents quickly, which ultimately eliminates a great deal of back-end administration. This advantage positions us to become one of the greatest and "greenest" life insurance companies in business today; when it comes to underwriting, we truly are an industry leader. Our systems can hit three different databases within two minutes— motor vehicle records, prescription drug records, and medical information—to make informed decisions and conduct effective underwriting of insurance policies.

The Human Touch

I believe the key to our success is that we have more than 90,000 licensed representatives in North America representing Primerica. Many companies have chosen to eliminate client home visits; we did not. Instead, we made the commitment to send our representatives into prospective clients' homes with technology that would enable them to do their jobs at the kitchen table. We do not want to eliminate our sales force; we want to empower them and grow distribution.

With all the advertising, people may be surprised that today fewer than 4 percent of life insurance policies are purchased through direct mail or over the Internet. This business depends on educating and informing clients, so we want to make sure our representatives are able to speak with these individuals, one-on-one, in the comfort of their own living rooms, dining rooms, and kitchens, sitting face-to-face with them over coffee, to help them determine the best life insurance policy for their situations.

Differentiating the Brand

At Primerica, we show up on Main Street in towns across North America, and we deliver financial services—principally term life insurance and savings and investment products—to the middle market, which we define as having household income between $30,000 and $100,000. This is one of the major ways we differentiate ourselves from the competition. The vast majority of financial service companies are structured in such a way that economics dictate that they focus primarily on the wealthy.

We also pride ourselves on our more measured approach. We do not wish to pressure anyone into buying our policies; rather, we aim to educate them about what they may need or can afford. We want to teach them about how to invest for the long term and how even a few dollars a month in savings can accumulate into large amounts over time. We want our clients to eliminate or restructure debt or save for a college education.

We also offer a complimentary, confidential financial need analysis that provides them with a great roadmap of where they are today and what steps they need to achieve their future financial goals. We do thousands of those a month, while most of our competitors charge anywhere from $500 to $3,000 for this service. Our decision to offer this tool free of charge goes a long way in showing our client that we are truly here to help them. Our goal is to provide them with life insurance products that give them the maximum coverage when they need it most. Finally, we pride ourselves on delivering on claims quickly. In fact, 92 percent of death claim benefits are delivered within two weeks.

Message Development

Communication plays a critical role at Primerica. Our representatives are independent contractors, and 90 percent of them work on a part-time basis. In short, they are a volunteer army.

Instead of sales quotas, we run dynamic and motivating sales contests, where those who compete and win get to go to dream destinations, such as Hawaii, the Atlantis resort, and many other places. In February 2012, the contest winners stayed at the Waldorf Hotel and had exclusive "ownership" of the awesome Universal Studios for one special night. We also use other means to keep them motivated and excited. Since 1986, we have owned and operated our own TV studio, which allows us to broadcast live to agents across North America using our own production materials. We recently upgraded to high definition, and we now stream all videos, both live and production videos, directly to our agent intranet portal. We call it Primerica Online Live (POL), and we have an in-house publications department staffed with about twenty graphic artists and writers who create all of our sales literature and brochures. We are also evolving our social media strategy, trying to figure out how we can help it enhance our message.

Marketing Message

Our marketing message is simple. We want to be known as the company that helps Main Street North America achieve financial independence. More than 68 million people in the United States have no life insurance at all. That is just heartbreaking. Moreover, another 50 million people say that they need more life insurance and that the death of the breadwinner would be tragic.

The average age of the North American life insurance agents is fifty-eight years old. Twenty years ago, the insurance industry wrote 20 million policies a year; now it writes only 10 million, and those policies that actually are in force are greatly reduced, as the following charts illustrate. Primerica sees itself as a company that can step in and deliver significant growth in the mainstream markets.

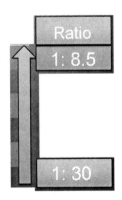

Reach Out and Touch Someone

We are so far ahead of the curve that in the upcoming year, we plan simply to refine our business model. However, we do plan to focus on helping our end users with their use of our technology. On one hand, some of our clients were given toy cell phones in their cribs, and technology is practically second-nature to them; on the other hand, some of our clients are still struggling to figure out how regular cell phones work. Consequently, we are invested in creating technology that captures the preferences of our end users.

Currently, we take a comprehensive approach, distributing our messages through multiple channels. We send them via the US Postal Service, fax them, post them on the public Internet site www.primerica.com, POL, e-mail them, and text them. That way, we will hit every user in every generation. In the future, we want to fine-tune this process and make sure that people are not receiving the same message in multiple forms. For instance, if they want to receive messages only via text, then that will be the only way they receive them. We want to be more personable in our approach, more proactive in understanding our end user, and more mindful of how we reach our different constituents.

Upcoming Challenges

The biggest challenge for us is growing our sales force. Today, if you look across North America, each state has different regulations and different exams. We are being very proactive in developing our system to grow distribution.

The other challenge is meeting market needs. As I mentioned previously, the middle income market is vastly underserved. The average household income for our clients is $67,000, which is close to the nationwide average. We go into our clients' homes, and we provide appropriate life insurance protection that will help them in the event of the tragic death of a breadwinner. We are not there to set up protection for estate planning tax purposes. Rather, our representatives help clients learn about savings against debt. There is a reason banks give kids lollipops and candy—because if you put $500 in a bank account at one percent for sixty-five years, it grows to roughly only $800. The bank wins! However, if you invest that same $500 at 10 percent or 12 percent, you wind up with $800,000 to $1.2 million. We try to educate our clients about how to plan properly for the future so they are equipped to make the best decisions about their money.

Key Takeaways

- Do not be quick to follow industry trends if doing so does not make sense to your business model.
- Although technology and the Internet seem like an effective tool to expedite delivery and reduce overhead costs, it is important to understand both the nature of your product and the habits of your clients to determine whether going digital is truly the right decision.
- Marketing is about educating your clients. Take the time to help them through complicated decisions; provide them with the tools they need; and have confidence in your product. If you can earn the trust of potential clients, you can also earn their business.

Duane M. Morrow is executive vice president of marketing for Primerica and chief marketing officer for Primerica Life. He joined Primerica in 1987 as a retirement planning clerk in the mutual funds division. He was promoted to positions of increasing responsibility over the next several years, and, in 1992, was named director of National Securities Marketing. After a successful three years as director, he was named vice president of marketing for Primerica-New York. In June of 1997 he was promoted to executive vice president of marketing and spearheaded the creation of a regional marketing division for the entire United States. The two-and-a-half years in this position also involved living in Los Angeles for one-and-a-half years.

In the next six years, Mr. Morrow was instrumental in opening Europe for Primerica under the banner of CitiSolutions, first, as head of marketing for Spain, later as country head of the UK. While living and working in the UK, he broke his neck playing rugby. He was given a 99 percent chance of never walking again. He has overcome those odds and now walks 99 percent of the time.

A native of Reynolds, Georgia, Mr. Morrow is a 1986 graduate of Norcross High School in Atlanta and Oxford (USA) University with a BA in marketing. He and his wife Kim and their five children currently reside in Hoschton, Georgia.

Crafting a Message That Resonates with Your Audience and Drives Business Results

Patricia L. Cluff

Associate Vice President,
Strategic Relations and Marketing
University of Virginia Health System

ASPATORE

Introduction

At times, marketers may choose to focus on the message without carefully considering business needs and the desired results from executing that message. However, it is important to realize that in most cases, the success of this message depends on first understanding the business needs and desired results. I remember seeing a television ad a few years back for obstetrics; the message was engaging, humorous, heartfelt, and memorable. Unfortunately, while the ad resonated with the audience on an emotional level, it did nothing to drive business. This was a valuable lesson.

At the academic medical center where I work, we were fortunate to be able to take a "deep dive" to first understand our market position and what it would take to improve preference—and ultimately increase market share. We conducted qualitative and quantitative consumer research, employee engagement, and physician satisfaction studies. Through this process, we learned a few things about ourselves and what we wanted to convey when developing our message.

First, we realized that building preference for female consumers required a different tone and message. Although communicating about external awards, new technologies, and the credentials of our recruited faculty and staff would help us build our *image*, to build *preference*, we needed to talk about things that actually resonated with consumers. We needed to answer their question, "What's in it for me?"

Second, we recognized that all faculty and staff play an important role in marketing our clinical programs, and we needed a better understanding of their views and perspectives. As with most, if not all, health care providers, we discovered that our employees are, in fact, our frontline marketers. We learned that "shrubbery talk" from employees, whether in the back yard, at a soccer game, or on a social media network, is far more telling than any other voice in the environment. Although this was not a traditional prioritization, we decided we needed to target our messaging to a different audience—our staff.

It was important that employees felt a sense of pride and remembered why they chose to work in an academic medical center. Our staff came here to learn, succeed, be challenged, and make a difference. We needed to reflect and embrace new stories to change our internal and external voices through our staff. As a result, we made a firm commitment to communicate, educate, and inform people in new and different ways. This past year, we continued our internal communications, but extended our work-to-service lines to reinforce our brand promise and differentiation in the marketplace.

Gauging Brand Perception

To gauge brand perceptions, we conduct annual quantitative consumer research, monitor patient satisfaction, and assess our employee engagement. In each case, we identify what the measure is and monitor performance over time.

For consumers, we continue to monitor awareness and image; however, building preference is the activity that will address our business need. We monitor distinct measures over time to understand our performance, and this requires both leading and lagging indicators. For example, in our case, if consumer preference increases, it is a leading indicator for patient volume growth.

Internally, we monitor our employees' sense of pride regarding their work for our health system. Externally, we monitor employees' likelihood to refer family and friends to the health system. As a result of our annual studies, we know that our employees have an increased sense of pride working in the system, and they are also more willing to refer family and friends to us for care.

From a patient perspective, we monitor overall satisfaction and loyalty to our health system. We never lose sight that, in addition to our employees, our patients are another source of brand promise, and they have a significant impact on whether we fulfill our promise or fall short. We are seeing improvements in distinct clinical areas. Our strengths are the spine, heart, and cancer-related issues.

Our referring physician data is much harder for us to obtain, but we have found that their overall satisfaction and self-reporting of referrals have improved, as well.

As a general rule that can apply to any marketer in any industry, to truly gauge brand perception, marketers must constantly monitor the marketplace. There is no one single input that will tell the full story. And while it takes time to build brand perception, it can take merely one moment to crush it. We have distinct strategies in place to improve brand perception, and performance measures are indispensable in this process.

Developing the Right Message

As previously mentioned, we determined that our business need was to build preference, which would ultimately increase market share. Through our research, we identified key messages that aligned with our vision, values, and culture and then tested them in focus groups consisting of previous patients, patients of our competitors, consumers, and employees.

The messages were evaluated on three key points:

1. Were they meaningful to the audience?
2. Were they believable for our health system?
3. Would they likely change target audience behavior?

With this knowledge, our advertising agency was able to develop a marketing and creative strategy. The marketing communications team could begin to integrate these messages through communications in writing, speeches, presentations, and so forth. In sum, we had established the connection between our business needs and the message that was required to achieve our business goals. And, over time, we have demonstrated the capacity to move our target audiences and achieve our desired improvements in preference and in utilization. We focused on engaging people in new and different ways, so that when they were at the point of making a decision, we were at the top of their minds.

Prioritizing Marketing Strategies

Defining your business needs, knowing your message, and understanding its desired impact on target audiences helps marketing create the right strategies for the organization. While we see distinct changes in our communication channels, it is important to realize that new messaging will not necessarily replace existing ones. The imperative is to understand how the new messages build on the older messaging that had already been established.

From our perspective, we have targeted, distinct strategies that all connect in meaningful ways. As an example, we have traditional advertising for our heart center that differentiates our expertise and capabilities from those of other providers in the marketplace and generates an emotional connection to our health system. Additionally, we have an affinity program that focuses on caring for a healthy heart that engages women through a distinct web center, events, and educational offerings. From there, we focus on our consumer magazine by featuring distinct stories and inviting others to join the affinity program. We also advance our consumer website and online advertising to pull our story together in a cohesive manner. In essence, we prioritize strategies that align and advance our engagement and dialogue.

Measuring the Impact of a Message

It is important to establish performance measures based on the means of measurement. Our annual consumer phone survey, employee engagement survey, and ongoing patient satisfaction measurement serve us well. Every other year, we conduct focus groups to garner more qualitative insights.

At the end of the day, we are here to enhance our reputation and to optimize our market share. Everything we do has a line of sight to that purpose, so the measures become easy and are dependent on the audience. We just need to make sure we measure consistently over time to demonstrate our performance accurately. While market share is our ultimate goal, at the same time, it is not something we have complete control over. We need good partners in operations to ensure that the patients have a positive experience, and it is an ongoing journey.

Changes in Message Development

A brand promise should rarely change. If it does, it might likely be a "flavor" versus a promise. However, how the message is developed will evolve over time. Initially, our primary focus was to improve our internal sense of pride and willingness to refer family and friends to our patient care services. This has evolved to getting all of our consumers to speak in a way that increases their listeners' preference and utilization. But, as a baseline, you will continue to see thematic alignment over time and over communication channels that cohesively build and reinforce your message.

Social Media and Mobile Technologies

Social media have played an increasingly important role in our marketing and communication strategies. We are in an environment where we can use a spectrum of tools and technologies, but we seek to be purposeful in our engagement. We do not launch "the next best tool"; just because we can does not necessarily mean we should. If, however, we find that a particular tool creates alignment to our business need and can advance our work, then we will certainly leverage it to accomplish our goals.

Moreover, it is important to recognize that different audiences will embrace technologies at different levels. My mother still wants a printed magazine, but my niece wants an application. Both are important, but as target audiences, their fulfillment of our business needs is different.

Understanding the technology and the industry is critical. While I personally struggle to join the twenty-first century, I push myself to adopt the technology. It is a brave new world out there. As an industry, we must embrace and understand its strengths and limitations. Whenever possible, we should seek to make the technology work for us, versus the other way around.

I see some organizations that are using every piece of technology they can get their hands on, but they do not know what it is doing for them or how it connects. Others are not doing it at all because they still have policies in their environment where you are not allowed to have a Facebook page. I would say we are somewhere in the middle, where we are trying to tread water and find the floor of the ocean to make sure we can actually stand up and get this done. We are choosing to deal with technology in a thoughtful manner, rather than being quick to do it just because we can.

Leveraging Opportunities for Free Publicity

The public relations and marketing area is changing significantly in our organization, and there are many reasons for it. Eight years ago, we had a public relations (PR) office that served more as media relations than anything else. Marketing and communications operated in a separate office. We would ping-pong ourselves between each other when meeting with 600 physicians with a variety of needs. It was not an effective system because PR would go in one day, and marketing would show up the next, and we would all be pointing fingers at each other and claiming that certain issues should have been handled by the other group.

Thankfully, this model changed a year ago, and we have now integrated the marketing and PR professionals. At this point, the focus is all about developing content that can be deployed to individuals who will use it within their own communication vehicles. Today we live in an environment where there are only a few reporters out there. When I first got here, there was a real desire to be referenced outside our state to gain a national reputation. We focused on national reporters, rather than local ones. Within the past year we realized that if we made it into our local paper, then three days later it would likely be in the capital city's paper, and then in a national paper after that, assuming the story had appropriate merit. Staying focused at home makes much more sense because of the way that business and industry work today.

Industry Challenges

Some of the more recent challenges we have been facing in this industry relate to market consolidations and health care reform. In the past, a marketer would be looking to fill that hospital bed; in the future, we will be thinking about how to keep the patient out of the bed. As we make that transition, we will need to live in both worlds for a time. In balance, four million additional people will have health insurance by 2014, and they will be given a choice of where to receive medical treatments. It is up to us to find a way to retain those patients. I think we need to continue to be curious in trying new media to understand what can be leveraged and how without losing sight of what we are trying to accomplish and whom we are trying to accomplish it with, and doing it in a meaningful way.

We as health care providers need to understand that the today's consumer cannot decipher the difference between one provider and another. We must distinguish our "product" and our message in a way that will help the consumer become more informed and educated in the decision-making process.

The other thing—which is true for most health systems—is that many of us are partnering with others, and one of our challenges is understanding how to communicate in such a way that the patient and the patient's family clearly understand from whom they are receiving care. Marketers will be challenged in building local brands, with affiliated brands, and/or being integrated into a new brand through acquisition.

Conclusion

Though every industry has its own nuances, creating an effective marketing strategy is all about strong market research. Marketers must understand what they want to accomplish and what performance metrics will track the appropriate results. If I am trying to build awareness, I am going to do X, Y, and Z, and if I am trying to grow volumes, I am going to do A, B, and C. Note that these actions are not the same.

As an example, we used to use a model that focused on building awareness, so consumers knew we existed. We thought the more we improved our image, the more likely we would improve patient preference. However, the reality is that building preferences is different from building image. We thought if we just kept doing what we were doing, we would in fact achieve our goals, but in the end, we had to reconstitute our work. Ultimately, if you do not know what you are trying to accomplish, you will inevitably struggle. As one of my mentors says, if you do not know where you are going, any road will get you there.

Key Takeaways

- Remember your front line marketers among your employees. It is important that the employees have a sense of pride in their jobs because they are among the best marketing tools available.
- Creating an effective marketing strategy requires market research, performance metrics, and an understanding of what you are trying to accomplish.

- Utilizing technology is necessary; however, it is important to choose only the most useful tools. Make sure everything has at least some sort of return.

- Finding the appropriate voice is a journey: continuously gauge your effectiveness with your audience to ensure you tell them what they want to hear without over-promoting.

Patricia L. Cluff is the associate vice president for marketing and strategic relations for the University of Virginia Health System. The Health System includes the University of Virginia (UVA) Medical Center, UVA Children's Hospital, Schools of Medicine and Nursing, UVA Physicians Group, and the Claude Moore Health Sciences Library. Ms. Cluff oversees market research and planning; market strategy and communications; and physician, public, and community relations. As part of her leadership in community relations, she currently serves as vice chair for the Charlottesville Regional Chamber of Commerce and as a board member for the Charlottesville Free Clinic and Thomas Jefferson Area Coalition for the Homeless. In addition, Ms. Cluff serves as the executive liaison to the UVA Hospital Auxiliary on behalf of the vice president and chief executive officer of the UVA Medical Center. She has been a member of the Health System administration since November 2002.

Prior to joining the UVA Health System, Ms. Cluff served in leadership positions at Premier Health Alliance, representing one-third of the United States hospitals, the University of Kentucky Chandler Medical Center, the University of North Carolina Health System in Chapel Hill, and Shands Healthcare at the University of Florida. While at the University of Kentucky, Ms. Cluff was recognized as the "young marketer of the year" by the Alliance for Healthcare Marketing.

Ms. Cluff holds EdS and master's degrees from the University of Florida in Gainesville and a bachelor's degree from Stephens College in Columbia, Missouri.

Building a Foundation for Your Offerings: Getting the Message Right

Seth Nesbitt

Chief Marketing Officer

Ecova

ASPATORE

Introduction: Messaging as an Executive Team Priority

My role as chief marketing officer at Ecova comprises two areas: everything associated with traditional marketing—corporate communications, events, and marketing programs—and product marketing/management—naming, positioning, pricing, requirements, feature definition, and go-to-market strategy.

When I joined Ecova, it had recently completed several major acquisitions and was supporting multiple brands while executing a strategic shift in focus. Messaging was a high-priority topic at the executive team level—messaging for the company, messaging for our offerings, messaging in general. There were fundamental questions everyone agreed needed to be answered about how we defined ourselves, our business, and our market space.

So we set out to do a total brand refresh that ended up including a new name and set of messages for the company, our key market segments, and our major market offerings. This was a great professional experience and a chance to use some of the tools and skills I had developed in over fifteen years marketing in the business-to-business (B2B) technology space. This chapter outlines the process we used and some of the key strategies we put into practice.

Not every company will see messaging as such a strategic priority. We were in a unique situation supporting two brand names in a relatively undefined market. But whether or not you are in as dynamic a situation as we were, messaging *should* be a high priority. Good messaging gets to the core of who you are as a company, helps you differentiate yourself from your competitors, and communicates to the market what you want to be known for. It can also have a powerful internal effect, increasing employee loyalty and aiding recruiting.

How Messaging Shapes Your Company's Story and Others' Perception

Ecova is a fast-growing company in a rapidly evolving space: energy management software and services. For us, messaging needed to answer some fundamental questions:

- What is our market?
- What is it called?

- What is the core value we deliver for clients?
- What are our differentiators?

Going through a messaging exercise enabled us to crystallize and clarify these key notions of who we are and provided a foundation for all our marketing and go-to-market efforts.

If you are entering a new market, targeting a new audience, or working on a new solution, messaging can provide a common framework of ideas and concepts to link your activities. It creates a common set of words for use in the market about who you are, what you are doing in this space, and how you can help customers.

The Link between Your Brand and Your Messaging

Messaging is the primary way you crystallize your differentiation—the things you want clients and prospects to know about you—so it is important to mention the link between messaging and branding. A good general definition of brand I like to use is "the collection of perceptions about you in the marketplace." It takes into account everything out there, what people think about you, and what they associate with your company and its products and services.

Since messages play a central role in defining what we want to be known for, your messaging platforms and differentiating statements put into motion a set of ideas, concepts, and attributes that will be associated with your brand. Differentiators are therefore critical to breaking through; it is important to ensure these are captured in your messaging and serve to set your company and brand apart.

Getting the Message Right: Focus on Value

Our view at Ecova, and my previous experience, is that messaging is best done comprehensively, starting with your top-level messages and then reaching down to support product-based, vertical, and segment-based messages. We also believe strongly that messages should be centered on the notion of delivering value to the customers. Those with a product marketing background (as I have) sometimes get caught up in the notion that your messages should be about your products, how great they are, and their features and functions. That can sometimes be true: depending on the product, your messaging can be tied to its unique capabilities, but messages have the most impact when they are built around the notion of value delivered to the client. Be sure they answer questions like "What does this mean to me?" and "How does this benefit my business/job/role?"; otherwise, your message will be tuned out if it is perceived as just another vendor talking about itself.

Messaging Ownership and Involvement

It is almost always true that the marketing department leads message development—runs messaging workshops, drafts the messages, gathers feedback, makes revisions, and is responsible for the final deliverable. Marketing is not the only stakeholder, but we are the pivot point in the process. In fact, as we revamped our messages at Ecova, we tried to have as many stakeholders as possible involved with message development, but we, in marketing, owned the process and the final outcome.

As the following illustration shows, within marketing, there are a number of options as to who should run, or "own," messaging—Product Marketing, Marketing Programs, Corporate Communications?

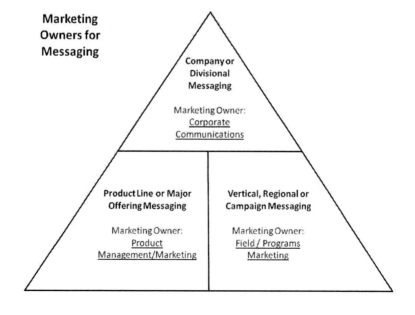

If you are a very large company, you may have a dedicated resource to help with message development, but usually it is a part-time responsibility of someone. At the highest level of messaging (all-company or large business unit) the most logical group is corporate communications, as they will be a primary user of the messages (for exec-level presentations, speaking opportunities, press releases, internal communications, etc.)

Others in the marketing group will get more involved as you go down to the next level of messaging. For example, product management/marketing is the likely "owner" of product- or solution-level messaging. For vertical or segment messages, programs or field marketing is a logical "owner." They will be responsible for the vehicles the messaging will ride on (campaigns, targeted events, etc.), and they have a vested interest in getting the message "right."

So if marketing owns the process, and corporate communications, product management, and programs marketing are the likely participants from marketing, who else should be involved? Messaging is a bit like corporate strategy. It is often best to have a mix of senior executives, as well as frontline employees involved. So when we pick individuals who will be involved in the messaging process, we may have C-level executives, as well as managers. We are also sure to ask people to participate who know the customers and the sales cycle well—usually people from the sales and client management organizations.

And while marketing drives the development of the message, as a general rule, if any group has veto power over messaging (such as the lead of a division or business unit), it should be involved, or you run the risk of not getting buy-in to roll out your messages.

It is also important to be as open about the messaging process as you can. Do not be secretive—let people know you are looking at revising your messaging. Share freely your plans: roughly how long it will take and who will be involved and how. This ensures the largest group—even people who are not on the core team—feels bought in and knows what is coming.

Developing Your Messages

The Workshop

The central activity for Ecova around developing our messaging was a messaging workshop. This has been my experience at previous companies, as well. There just doesn't seem to be another way to get to a good set of messages other than getting a group of people together in a room for an extended period. For a major exercise, such as messaging for an entire company, or for a major market offering, this typically requires a half-day to full-day exercise where a cross-functional team comes together and attempts to identify the most important messages and pull them together into a draft. I recommend a minimum of five participants and not more than a dozen.

And while the workshop is central, and most of the work has to happen there, I recommend doing some pre-work to make the most effective use of your time in-person. This can be a questionnaire distributed via e-mail. The pre-work should not be directly about the messages—that can come in the workshop. It is questions about the market, what is going on with customers, why you are winning, and what people are saying about you and your competitors. These insights are then used to develop messages in the workshop.

The goal of the workshop should be to get you 80 percent to 90 percent of the way there. Messaging is a process that can span from a few weeks to several months. Great messaging can rarely be done in one day and needs input from a larger group. Ideas need to settle, and after an intense burst of creativity, sometimes, valuable refinements can emerge.

What Does Good Messaging Look Like?

For a companywide initiative or major business unit, the messaging exercise outcome should be a comprehensive message map usually several pages or slides long. This should include top-level messages, as well detailed supporting points. It should include market-ready statements that can be directly lifted and then used in a variety of ways, including web content, campaigns, sales tools, and presentations. Good messaging answers the major questions of what sector you are in, what value you bring, and what differentiates you. One tool for these top-level messages I have used in the past is a Messaging House Framework. It goes beyond simple benefits statements and helps flesh out your messages into usable elements.

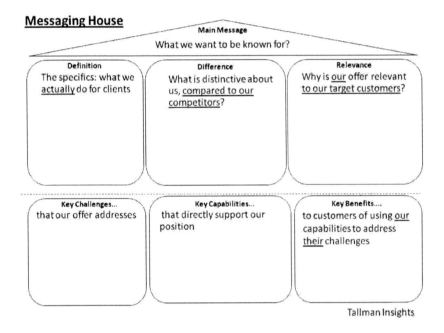

Tallman Insights

Message Map

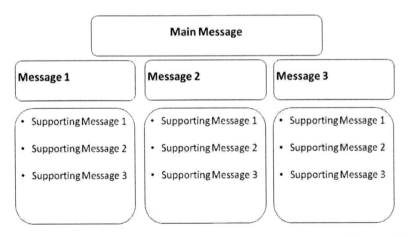

Tallman Insights

In my experience, messages for product lines and vertical/segment audiences can be less intensive—developed by a smaller group in less time. The outcomes from these can be simpler message maps focused on the key benefits and differentiators of a particular product or service.

Regardless of the scope of the exercise, a common mistake is to get too detailed and go to deep. Do not make the mistake of taking four months trying to perfect the message for a particular offering or segment. You would be better off spending four weeks with a small target team, coming up with some messages, and then market-testing them. The only time I have seen a messaging exercise go much longer and be worth it is when detailed supporting points are being developed—proof points on why the messaging and value statements are true. This can take time if none exists and is worth the effort.

In Person versus Online

If you work in a geographically dispersed company (as many are these days), the question inevitably comes up about whether you need an in-person meeting for the workshop. While video-conferencing technology is getting better, given the strategic importance of message, it is worth spending the time to have an in-person meeting. I have found there truly is no substitute for getting into the same office and sitting around a conference table and working on messages. Being able to see the reactions and to read the body language of participants is important if you want to get the best message and buy-in from the participants.

Pros and Cons of Working with Vendors to Craft Your Message

To facilitate the messaging process, some people turn to outside vendors. This has worked well for me in the past, particularly with strategic messaging or when the messaging is across a broad section of products and audiences. When we are doing that type of broad work, it helps to have an outside person provide a sanity check. This individual will let you know whether your messaging will resonate with the broader market, and if you are using too many acronyms or insider language. He or she will encourage you to talk in plain terms and home in on the differentiators. When entering new markets, a vendor can also be helpful in reviewing your story and terminology to make sure it is relevant to potential customers. He or she will also be able to provide difficult feedback to stakeholders, if needed, in a way that peers may not be able to.

But vendors do have limitations. What a vendor cannot do is know your space as you do. Sometimes an outside vendor just cannot get up to speed quickly enough, and while vendors add value, there may be too steep a learning curve. This is often the problem with technical products being sold to a technical audience.

Another aspect of working with vendors that can be problematic is cost. Let's say you are launching a major messaging initiative. If you start with overall company messaging and extend that across six or eight business units and four or five major verticals, the process can become very expensive. What has worked for me in the past is to work with a vendor on the top-level messages for the company or business unit and then utilize internal teams for the next level down of messages. This works well, as the top-level messages are most likely to be seen by the broadest group—press, analysts, influencers, et al. The next level down of messaging is likely to be more buyer-specific, and your internal teams can best know this detailed information.

Another point on working with vendors: when possible, choose someone with experience in your space. I have worked with Tallman Insights (www.tallmaninsights.com) for many years on multiple engagements. Its focus is developing messaging for complex B2B technology offerings. This is all the company does, and because it does this all the time, it does it very, very well. Note that virtually any marketing support firm can do messaging well—it does not have to be a specialist firm. It just needs to have the relevant experience. Public relations (PR) firms, branding agencies, and strategic consultancies are all possible choices—the type of vendor firm is less important than whether it has true competence with messaging. Ask to see samples; check references and make sure they have the relevant experience.

So, in general, I believe vendors are especially helpful with high-level messaging and when it is at a global level across regions and audiences. I think vendors begin to lose value as you become more detailed in your messages around particular solutions or audiences.

Measuring the Impact of Your Messages

Depending on the size of your company, different methods for measuring messaging impact make sense. The most trustworthy I have seen are certain types of awareness surveys. Ask people to name a leader or company who is representative of a certain attribute you want to be aligned with key attributes of your brand (most reliable, most secure, most effective, etc.). Do the same survey over a period of months (or years) to understand the impact of your messages. However, there is one major drawback with this approach—it is expensive. Another is that it is that awareness surveys can take time to reflect changes and do not give immediate feedback because changes in perception can take time to filter through surveys.

For immediate feedback, try using customer surveys. You can ask questions about specific attributes of the company that are included in your messaging and see how the results change over a much shorter period. I have used this method in the past to get feedback on whether customers rate us highly on the attributes we are trying to promote in our messaging.

It is also important to assess the degree to which your messaging gets used by sales, people inside the organization, and even customers. There is nothing better than seeing your chief executive officer (CEO) or other senior leadership in action with employees and clients using the messages you shape for the market. If it is useful and used in those settings, it is a message that resonates. It is a soft measure, but certainly valuable.

Another indicator of success with messaging is whether the market begins to pick up elements of your messages. When you see customers, industry experts, and analysis using your terminology and your way of describing the market challenges, that is a good sign of success.

The Evolution of Messaging across Media

Message development and usage has undergone an evolution, though not a revolution. There is a pretty standard set of tools around messaging—

message maps and documents. I would venture that if you look at messaging documents from five or even ten years ago, the changes will be minor. But the media for carrying your messages have changed.

Website

In the B2B space, a company's website is likely one of the most important vehicles for its messages. It is the "front door" for virtually everyone who interacts with your company—prospects, clients, job seekers. So it needs to be laid out in way that allows people to see your messages both on the home page and several levels down. And good messaging content that is shorter and direct tends to work well on the web, as people are not reading lengthy blocks of text anymore.

One thing to take into account is that websites need to be much more interactive these days. So it is important to think about how your messages can be included in things like video case studies and demos. Interactive content infused with your message is a much more effective way to use the web and pull people in than masses of text on a page.

Social Media

I am a big fan of social media, which we are using at Ecova. I was also a champion for it at my previous company—a great vehicle for communications. When you use social media, the best approach is to use your messages by association, rather than communicating them directly. Say, for example, that one of your important messages is around the notion of data or data security, and this is the primary way that your business provides value to your customers. Your participation in social media should be in conversations about data and security. You can contribute when the topic comes up in different forums. Find the data security sites, and start following the data security influencers; look for an article that calls out the benefits of good data security; share your comments; and then share links to your site. Use social media as a vehicle for association to tie back to your message. Cutting and pasting your messages into Twitter or onto forums will succeed only in turning people off. You need to participate in conversations over social media to properly use it.

Some very sophisticated companies are doing great things with social media, but we are still in the early days. The majority of companies are just looking to reposition their marketing messages over social media. We have not found that to be the most effective approach because people are becoming experts at tuning out vendor messages—in social media and elsewhere. Buyers are getting hit with so many messages these days that their first reaction is to tune it out if it appears as overt marketing. The key is to find a way to use the power of association and participation through social media to get your point across.

Public Relations

A book called *The Fall of Advertising and the Rise of PR* by Al Ries and Laura Ries was published in 2002, shortly after the dot.com era, when companies had spent huge amounts on advertising. The book pointed out that some of the most successful companies were hardly spending any money advertising (Starbucks, e.g.), but were taking advantage of great PR. Admittedly, for some sectors this approach will not work. If you sell certain types of consumer goods, you need to be heavily involved in advertising. But for many people, the ideas presented in the book helped them realize PR was a more effective way to raise your profile and get people talking.

In the B2B energy and sustainability space, there is a heavy emphasis on thought leadership. If we want to take advantage of the power of PR, we need to develop thought leadership around trends and topics and capitalize on it. We find topics and trends that are interesting to buyers and are related to our key messages. Since these people are interested in the topic, they are not actively tuning it out, so we have an opportunity to expand on our messages in a thought leadership format. We do not say, "Here are our products," but, rather, "Here is an industry challenge; this is our take on it; and this is why you should be interested in us." Some people refer to this as "content marketing."

For example, maybe we will do a white paper that has important information in the industry. It is not tied to our product, but we have created a report or survey and captured interest. People notice who has put the information out there and listen to the message. They keep that in mind when looking for companies that can solve their business problems.

Advertising

Although we are doing more with our website and in the social media environment, it is important to state that we use traditional media, such as advertising; it has not gone away. We are not a big advertiser, and you will not see us doing television spots or placing ads in newspapers, but we are selectively involved in industry publications and see them as important venues for our messages. They add value for us with those readers in different vertical sections and in specific buyer roles that we target from our customer base. We typically do a combination of print and online advertising (including search engine marketing) in conjunction with a campaign targeted at a particular audience.

Messaging in Action

Targeting Buyers and Influencers

One of the "big-picture" trends of the last ten years in marketing is that buyers are getting better at tuning out messages. Buyers are being bombarded by messaging across different platforms (online, mobile, print, etc.), and the higher you go in an organization regarding the purchase decision, the better the individuals are at tuning out "noise" from vendors. Thought leadership and content-based marketing, as mentioned above, is a key way to reach these decision makers with your messages.

Another valuable strategy is to build strong relationships with industry influencers—not just journalists and industry analysts, but consultants, bloggers, academics, and anyone else with a large following in a particular industry sector. If you can identify those influencers and build relationships with them, you can make sure they understand your message and the value and benefits you bring to potential clients. This will help you break through because, increasingly, buyers are looking to the influencers to help guide them in their purchase decisions.

Messaging: The Core Elements in an Effective Marketing Campaign

We have discussed how a company's website and PR strategy are powerful presenters of the top-level messages for your company. But at the next level down—product messages, vertical messages, etc.—the appropriate vehicle for messaging is through campaigns. If you have a particular audience, say retail store owners, it makes complete sense to build a set of messages for a particular campaign to target that particular audience. The campaign will produce measureable outcomes that can tell you directly whether your messages resonate (click-through, open rate, conversion). In this way, a good multichannel campaign gives your messaging something to ride on and is a great way to test the big message and sub-messages after already releasing them at a higher level.

Picking Your Shots: How Deep to Go

As mentioned above, one of our recent initiatives at Ecova was to recreate a top-level set of messages for the entire company. We have taken those messages down to the next level, to our key customer segments and major market offerings. This can be a never-ending process; you can always get more granular, down to an even lower level.

But there is a point of diminishing returns. While it is important to tailor your messages to your audience, you also cannot have unique messages for every region, vertical, and product. For example, earlier in my career, I was involved in a global marketing effort for a product that had presence in more than a hundred countries. The general manager said he wanted specific messages for the product by region, segment, and role. We had six regions, four market segments, and five target roles—chief financial officer, chief information officer, vice president of customer care, et al.). It would have been impossible to create distinct messaging maps for each of these audience groups (you would have needed 120!). So we had to pick and choose using educated guesses about logical groups and the best coverage—you cannot do it all.

Allow Customers to Spend Time with Your Message

Finally, one lesson I have learned is not to be in a rush to change messaging once it is in use. All too often, marketers come up with a set of messages, roll them out, and become tired of them in a few months because they have spent so much time with them. Marketers need to keep in mind that customers may have heard their messages only once or twice, and they have not even had time to sink in.

In marketing, we have the tendency to come out with a new set of messages before the last ones have set in. Higher-level messages, particularly ones that cross a broad number of user categories, need to be used for at least a year, if not longer. It takes a while for customers to get real exposure to them. This is true across business and consumer marketing, but maybe most difficult in B2B—it takes time to get the message through to your sales team and your channel partners.

More targeted messages aimed at a certain type of individual or developed for a specific campaign will have a shorter shelf life; those messages can mature every six to nine months or even sooner, depending on the length of the campaign. However, we still need to be sure we do not fall into the habit of regularly coming up with a new message and then virtually throwing it away. Always remember to reinforce your messages continually because it takes time for them to sink in.

Message Duration

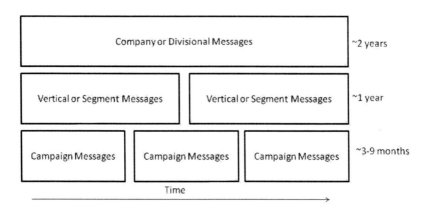

A quotation by Winston Churchill makes a great point on sticking with your messages:

> *If you have an important point to make, don't try to be subtle or clever. Use a pile driver. Hit the point once. Then come back and hit it again. Then hit it a third time—a tremendous whack.*

That is a great image for marketers. If you are the best at data or security or speed or savings or whatever, do not be subtle about it— bring it into everything you do. You will get tired of your messages before your customers do. Take care to re-use them and reinforce them every chance you get.

Conclusion

Having recently completed a major top-down messaging initiative at Ecova, I was amazed at the transformative effect it had on the entire organization. It has helped clarify our vision for the market and enabled us to articulate how we will continue to deliver on our mission statement. Our messaging helped unify the company and speed the integration process following a number of large acquisitions by giving us a unified story about us, our market, and the value we deliver that we can tell our clients and prospects, as well as each other.

I believe now, more than ever, that messaging can and should be a central pillar of a company's marketing efforts. I encourage you to take the time to focus on getting your core messages right. You will be glad you did.

Key Takeaways

- All messages should be centered on the notion of delivering value to the customers.
- The workshop is the key activity in message development. Be sure to include a mix of participants, from senior to front line, some of whom interact directly with customers.
- Consultants and vendors can be beneficial to the development of broad marketing messages because they can facilitate the process and help you avoid insider jargon.
- Assess the degree to which your messaging is used by sales, people inside the organization, and even customers.
- Buyers are growing better at tuning out messages. They are bombarded by messaging, and the higher you go in an organization regarding purchase decisions, the better the individuals are at tuning out vendors, so find influencers who can tell your story for you.

- You will get tired of your messages before your customers do. Re-use them and reinforce them, keeping in mind that your customer may have heard your message only once.

Seth Nesbitt is chief marketing officer of Ecova, an energy and sustainability management firm that uses technology-based solutions to help large commercial and industrial companies, as well as utilities, save resources. At Ecova, Mr. Nesbitt leads all aspects of marketing and product management, helping the company become the leader in total energy and sustainability management.

Mr. Nesbitt joined Ecova from Parallels Inc., a fast-growing cloud computing firm, where he led marketing for the company's B2B division. Prior to that, he was vice president of products and solutions marketing for Amdocs Inc., a $3 billion software and solutions provider for the telecommunications sector. Before that, he held field marketing and corporate communications positions at Nortel Networks, which was acquired by Amdocs.

Mr. Nesbitt holds a BA in history from Macalester College in St. Paul, Minnesota, and an MBA from Oxford University in Oxford, England. He is also a member of the North American Advisory Board for the CMO Council. When he is not working, he enjoys reading real books (not in electronic format), as well as hiking and fly-fishing with his wife and two children in the mountains and rivers of the Pacific Northwest.

Acknowledgment: *I would like to acknowledge the following individuals for their assistance over the years:*

- *Ed Gallagher, for giving me my first job in marketing*
- *Michael Matthews, for seeing my potential*
- *Mike Couture, for your patience and forbearance*
- *Guy Dubois, for teaching me the power of a message well delivered*
- *Jim Tallman, for showing me how real messaging is done*
- *Jeff Heggedahl, for leading in the style I aspire to*

Using Targeted Communications Strategies to Promote Brand Awareness and Build a Loyal Customer Base

John Leeman

Chief Marketing Officer

FreshDirect LLC

ASPATORE

Introduction

At FreshDirect, my team is responsible for all marketing, including strategy, new customer acquisition, loyalty, and eCommerce. Our team is also responsible for the revenue side of the profit and loss statement (P&L), sales and sales forecasting, and consumer segmentation and analytics.

Prior to working at FreshDirect, I was able to accumulate the expertise needed for the chief marketing officer (CMO) role in a combination of different positions. The most similar role to the one I am in today was a corporate marketing role at Hyperion Solutions (now Oracle). But the deepest experience I draw on is in brand positioning, advertising campaign development, and media communications planning. This was gained while working for global advertising and media agencies in the United States and China, advising clients like Procter & Gamble (P&G), Microsoft, American Express, Anheuser-Busch, and J&J.

Core Strategies for Communicating Key Differentiators to the Customer

This broad experience across many different business sectors and within multiple company cultures has helped me understand which aspects of marketing are truly fundamental and which are variable, based on the specific needs of each business or management style.

At FreshDirect, we are evolving our business model into one that is more market-centric versus operations-centric. My team has worked hard to understand which prospects and consumers are the most valuable. Using this information, we crafted a positioning and go-to-market strategy that leverages how we differ from the competition. Our primary strategic insight has been identifying the most powerful category and brand barriers for our specific consumer segments. We then leverage the barriers that can be overcome with marketing to maximize our trial and share opportunity.

To understand these segments and barriers we enlisted the help of different specialists; one in particular is Peter Krieg, president and chief executive officer (CEO) of Copernicus Marketing. Peter helped us develop a quantitatively based consumer segmentation model and a positioning strategy to leverage with the most valuable segments. This strategy is new to the company and has been quite helpful in quantifying our business opportunity and informing us how we can best reach the people that represent most profitable growth. We have also worked with consultants, such as Kate Newlin, who is the author of the book, *Shopportunity*. She is a retail marketing strategist who helped us identify many trial and loyalty barriers, which helped us in turn form our brand strategy and equity principles. The results of this research have since been transformed into our current marketing campaign.

Crafting Messages for All Audiences

FreshDirect's marketing messages have all been geared to appeal to different stakeholders—from consumers, employees, and suppliers to the media and the community at large. While our primary focus is to satisfy the needs of the buying customer, we think about all of our different constituents. We also want to make sure we are triangulating the needs of our local farmers and other gourmet or premium-quality food manufacturers so that we are leveraging their brands' positioning, too.

As we look to a new operational expansion in another part of New York City, we are also focused on ensuring that we are working in partnership with our surrounding community. We try to develop an overall company strategy that reflects our brand purpose of making our consumers' lives "one-stop simple" and helping them live every day to the fullest.

But everyone on our team needs a reason to come to work beyond just selling products and making profits. That is why our pilot program approved by the US Department of Agriculture (USDA) to help bring Food Stamps to moms and families who need the convenience of ordering healthy, fresh foods online as much as or more than some more affluent consumers serves as an inspirational example of FreshDirect's commitment to doing good.

Best Practices for Differentiating Our Brands

I am a strong proponent of the philosophy that P&G has recently made popular with its purpose-driven brands. We are working to crystallize this concept into our own future strategy and go-to-market plans. Developing purpose-driven brands is a powerful way to be relevant to customers, community members, and employees. They especially motivate those employees who want to pursue their passions at work and try to make a difference in the world. We feel that our chosen purpose should support our positioning and differentiation in the marketplace—and we try to make sure no other brand is living in the same space as our brand.

Effective marketing messages certainly play a large role in our brand development, but they also help when we go to market. We need to be able to articulate our brand purpose and the essence of what makes our brand different and superior in the eyes of consumers. We also want to be able to conduct programs and activities in the marketplace that align and support this same exact purpose. Consequently, we need to make sure that our corporate donations are focused on the charities and areas that are central to our purpose.

Measuring the Impact of Messaging

We measure the impact of our messaging in several ways: we measure it in sales, and we measure it in terms of the types of people we are able to convert into loyal customers. This latter one is a new and powerful metric for us, and one we are learning more and more about every day. Our consumer analytics group is constantly looking at how—and how much—our messages and promotional strategy resonate among the audiences we have identified as prime prospects. We are also going to measure awareness and the stickiness of our communications and marketing programs per dollar. We expect the stickiness to go up as the resonance and relevance of these messages increase. As we deploy and support this purpose-driven brand strategy, we also expect existing customers will demonstrate a higher level of awareness and brand advocacy and will help us acquire new customers via word-of-mouth marketing.

The returns on investment for an effective messaging strategy are many. The key ones will translate into high amounts of loyalty per dollar invested and a corresponding high valuation of our business in terms of investor value versus our competition. We believe that the more people value our position and purpose, the more they will be willing to pay a premium to support a company that represents that purpose versus another brand.

Evolution of Message Development Practices and Message Platforms

Message development practices have changed in the past five years; while the fundamentals may be the same, the need to be relevant and emotional is a huge lever we would like to explore further. Consumers now put a premium on brand authenticity and on the appropriateness of others speaking their minds and evangelizing our story for us. This is why we have developed a series of documentary-style shopper journey videos that show consumers how much effort and knowledge we apply to select the foods they can buy in our online store. We are also excited to deploy Bazaar Voice consumer reviews into our shopping experience, and we will leverage social media as a platform to promote both consumer reviews and our branded video content.

Leveraging "House Party" to Spread the Word about the FreshDirect Brand

One of the new communications methods we recently used was a social and experiential service called House Party (provided by HouseParty.com). House Party is a social media marketing platform that helps brands recruit influential individuals to throw Tupperware® Party-esque parties for a broad range of brands. The opportunity for us was to be able to take an influential group of prospective consumers through the awareness, consideration, trial, and evangelism phases of the "purchase funnel" all in one rich, engaging, social, at-home marketing experience.

Because we deliver fresh food to people's homes, our situation is a bit more challenging than that of most House Party customers who pack up a product sample and a curriculum to send out in boxes via mail. These brands can do thousands and thousands of House Parties in a single day because they just have to go to a third-party fulfillment center and send all of these packages out at once. For us, the fresh food cooked and beverages served at the House Party are actually our products we want them to try, which we need to deliver ourselves. So we need to integrate this into our overall ordering and delivery process. Still, it was scalable enough. Unfortunately, the control we were able to exert on the qualifications of the party hosts and guests was lower than we needed, and this program underperformed on our targets.

In summary, the core methods of creating an effective marketing message are a clear understanding of the consumers and their needs and a clear vision for how the company's brand benefits best meet those needs. Focusing on a positioning that drives directly to the heart of those long-lasting needs is a strategy that one must follow while at the same time de-prioritizing product claims and messages that are not paramount to the prime prospect. Finally, leveraging consumer communication channels that emphasize the brand benefits is the last piece of the puzzle.

Using Social Media and Mobile Technologies to Spread the Word

We leverage the social media channel and deploy it using a couple of strategies. When we first started revisiting our social media strategy during the summer of 2011, we had 1,700 Facebook fans. We needed to build our base community first. Today we have more than 30,000 Facebook fans, and our goal is to have 50,000. This is a significant group relative to our customer base. Now, it is about performance and value from this community. Our goal is to leverage community members who want to communicate through the social media channel for a wide array of purposes from customer service to promotions to referral programs.

As is the case with most company e-mail marketing programs, few of the recipients actually open and read marketing e-mails. Social media offer an opportunity for people who choose to integrate and engage in social media instead of e-mail. It also provides them a referral platform for amplification if they like what they hear and see. Our goal for building a social media channel is to locate an engaged audience that is paying attention to what we are doing and to augment other channels that are not social.

We also have a mobile application that is being widely adopted. Besides mobile applications, we have mobile browsers on tablets, and this use is increasing daily compared to that of other channels. Right now, more than 15 percent of our total transactions occur through those mobile devices, and mobile devices touch even more transactions at different points in the process. Our online grocery delivery service is unique in most eCommerce retail categories: customers actually build their orders all week long, adding items to their cart as they think of things they need.

Another quality that differentiates us is that we are able to provide some customer service and order delivery services through Facebook and Twitter. We recently employed a policy that allows our customer service groups to directly intercept comments and questions that relate to a delivery versus comments and questions that relate to our brands and merchandise. This capability has been helpful, providing consumers with another choice in how they want to engage with us. We are trying to meet customers where they want us to be with as many different ways to contact us as possible, and to ensure that their communications will be received by the right people in our company who will be able to answer their questions directly.

Evolution of the Company Website

Our company website is evolving. Initially we wanted it to share that our company provided the best overall experience for online shopping, and leverage our key differentiators and customized benefits that only an online grocery model like FreshDirect can actually deliver. For example, while other companies and stores try to leverage the ability to pick an item off a virtual shelf, we actually offer people the ability to customize just as if they were going to their local butcher shop or deli. Online, they can order steaks just as thick as they want and have them packaged in multiple ways. They can also order cheese and deli meats to be sliced thin, medium, or thick.

Our website evolved to provide this unique service. For the future, we are heading in a much more social direction that places more value on people's communities. So, while our website currently has a proprietary feature that gives advice from FreshDirect experts on the best fruits and vegetables before you buy them, we are going to build in customer reviews that will enable consumers to rank other kinds of products that are not fresh. They will be able to share their favorites and ultimately even build lists of these favorites they can refer to when they shop or share with new customers they bring in—our number-one source of new customers.

The Role of Traditional Media (and Free Publicity) in Marketing FreshDirect

We do, however, still use traditional media. Frequently, our messages are targeted at people who are not aware of us. We are quite clear on the key purchase barriers for the online grocery and delivery category. We like to leverage targeted communications, whether they are digital marketing sponsorships on websites to target audiences that fit our prime prospects or locally oriented communications (such as outdoor and transit advertising) that focus on those consumers who would most benefit from a premium online grocery delivery service. We still use these channels because getting people to come to our website before they know who we are or before we have overcome a couple of key purchase barriers for the category is often much more difficult to do using direct marketing alone than using a blend of direct and mass marketing. Once those barriers are overcome, we quickly move into offer-driven programs.

We leverage opportunities for free publicity through a number of different content strategies. The publicity about our products focuses tightly on how our merchandise is differentiated—for instance, because it is locally sourced, organic, or sustainable. Our YouTube channel (youtube.com/freshdirect) is a platform for a variety of equity-building branded content. We intend to leverage public relations (PR) and social media to monetize this content extensively. We also try to communicate key topics in a number of different places and with paid media. And when free publicity comes to us, we really try to get the truth out through those vehicles.

When releasing so much of the articulation of our communications to sources we do not fully control, there will inevitably be misstatements (by the brand or the media) and sometimes even mischaracterizations of what we believe to be true. If the company makes a mistake, our best-practice protocol is simply to apologize, clarify, and move forward quickly. We have armed our front lines of PR and customer service with the right kinds of information and have made sure they understand what the facts are so they can answers questions appropriately. We track exactly what is going on in the marketplace so we can understand where the negativity is coming from.

We try to focus the narrative on the right story versus the one that people on the extreme fringes of certain issues often try to spread.

Most of our customers see things in a balanced way, and we try to reflect that balanced view in our overall message so that it makes sense and connects to people in a way that will encourage them to share the same perspective. That way is not unlike our overall marketing communications, other than not being able to control the emotional element we try to build in our paid advertising.

Conclusion

Internet retailers are starting to adopt more sophisticated psychographic targeting principles to unlock value in overall store positioning, marketing tactics, and merchandising strategies. Social media, digital innovations, sophisticated database marketing solutions, and creative branded content and advertising can work together to drive high effectiveness and efficiency marketing.

Traditionally, Internet companies have focused on acquisition and initial public offerings (IPO) vs. long-term sustainable growth, but companies like FreshDirect are starting to evolve as leaders by applying significant investment in fundamentals and innovation to compete in a more challenging global marketplace.

Key Takeaways

- An effective overall branding strategy should reflect the higher social purpose of the company and brand while also leveraging the primary benefits of the product.
- With a purpose-driven brand strategy, existing customers can demonstrate a higher level of brand advocacy and help the company acquire new customers via word of mouth.
- Equity-building content can help illustrate a brand's purpose and inspire consumers to buy, media to amplify brand messages, and employees to be more creative and productive.

- Brands should focus on positioning that aligns with long-lasting needs and de-prioritize any messages that are not paramount to your prime prospect.

John Leeman, chief marketing officer of FreshDirect LLC, is responsible for brand strategy, all forms of paid, owned, and earned media, eCommerce technologies, sales forecasting, and business analytics. FreshDirect is the leader in gourmet grocery delivery and the largest online grocer in the United States, with customers in New York, New Jersey, and Connecticut. FreshDirect ranks seventy-fifth on Internet Retailer's Top 500 Guide®.

Previously, Mr. Leeman was the global American Express account lead at WPP media agency Mindshare. Before that, he led a communications planning team at Carat, New York, for Procter & Gamble's largest global brand Pampers®, a position he had held since 2006.

Prior to his roles in communications planning, Mr. Leeman spent sixteen years ascending to leadership roles within global creative agencies in New York, Shanghai, and San Francisco, developing integrated creative campaigns for General Mills, Anheuser-Busch, Microsoft, and Hyperion (now Oracle).

Originally from Kansas City, Mr. Leeman holds a BS in journalism from the University of Kansas. He lives in the financial district of Manhattan with his wife, Grace Hon.

Utilizing Brand Messaging to Develop Key Marketing Programs

Adam Chamberlain

Vice President, Marketing

Black Diamond Equipment

ASPATORE

Introduction

My title is vice president of marketing for Black Diamond Equipment (BD). Today's BD is the child of Chouinard Equipment, which was founded in 1957. Yvon Chouinard (who later founded his outdoor clothing business, Patagonia, in 1973) created a pioneering climbing hardgoods manufacturer focused on minimalist and highly functional designs for modern climbers and backcountry skiers. Chouinard Equipment was forced into bankruptcy in 1988 after a series of personal liability lawsuits. Led by the general manager of Chouinard Equipment, Peter Metcalf, a small group of employees purchased the company assets, changed the name to Black Diamond Equipment Ltd., and moved the business to Salt Lake City, Utah. Peter Metcalf continues to lead the company today. BD is one with the history of rock climbing, ice climbing, backcountry skiing, and mountain sports.

My role is to use this heritage, our latest innovative product developments, and our intimacy with mountain sports to develop inspiring, authentic, and innovative marketing materials that drive the business forward and engage our global community of climbers, skiers, and outdoor athletes. Our decentralized, yet global, marketing team consists of twenty marketing professionals in our Salt Lake City headquarters and ten marketing professionals at our European sales/marketing office in Reinach, Switzerland.

Engagement in Marketing Initiatives

We have driven three major marketing initiatives over the last five years— a shift from print to digital communication with consumers, development of a visual merchandising program as a core competence, and our evolution from purely product-based marketing tactics to a stronger brand marketing approach.

In 2008, we shifted from a print marketing-driven organization to a digital one. While the flagship of our marketing initiatives had been a brand-focused print catalog as a direct mail piece, we had largely ignored the growing audience for BD online. Seeing the writing on the wall, we redirected our strategy toward an online marketing initiative that would recreate BlackDiamondEquipment.com as the epicenter of our brand. In making this transition, we redesigned our website and began working hard at developing social media programs and laying the foundation for the full complement of a modern online marketing program. Ultimately, we completely moved away from end-consumer-facing print marketing collateral in an effort to deliver a more focused, high-quality, and powerful BD brand experience online to a much larger audience.

Impact of Increased Website Use on Demographics

Our reach and demographics have changed dramatically. We used to send our catalog to a house file that was fairly small, consisting of approximately 50,000 people. Now we have more than 90,000 fans on Facebook. Climbing enthusiasts who once connected with us exclusively via our printed catalog mailing twice a year now interact with us daily on our website, company blog (BD Journal), digital catalogs, and social outlets, including Facebook, Twitter, and Instagram. In North America alone, there are upwards of three million people climbing more than two times a year. Approximately 26 million mountain enthusiasts need durable, innovative gear to help them pursue their passion for being outside.

We will greet more than 2.5 million unique visitors in 2012. Many of these will be returning customers familiar with our brand, but more than 50 percent will be new customers, and the majority of these customers will be between eighteen and twenty-five years old and consume their media primarily through online channels. We are just beginning to tap the power of our analytics, to turn on customer relationship management (CRM) programs, and to contemplate the future of personalization through our online marketing channels.

Point-of-Purchase Fixturing

Our second major initiative has been the development of our retail marketing programs to include visual merchandising. At BD, product has always been king, so our inclination is to build best-in-class products first and let that product be the marketing, letting the product do the selling. This tactic works with a strong network of specialty retail partners and appeals to highly engaged consumers who have grown up with BD and believe in the brand. But as the specialty retail landscape has evolved, and retail floors have become even more competitive, point-of-purchase (POP) marketing materials have emerged as a requirement to raise our brand awareness and educate end consumers about the key features and benefits of our competitive product.

After a year-and-a-half of development and testing, we have built a strong program of branded items and fixtures to feature our products and to help retailers manage their inventory, but also to help them sell our diverse categories of products. In addition, this comprehensive visual merchandising program will pull together our diverse product categories with unified branding, highlight these categories, and do a better job of making the retailer feel like the significant Black Diamond Equipment dealer it is. Combined with the strong industrial design characteristics of our product line and well-branded packaging, the launch of this visual merchandising initiative in spring 2013 will improve brand awareness at retail and generate increased revenue for the retailer.

Transitioning from Product Focus to Brand Focus

Our third key initiative is our transition from a product-focused marketing organization to a product- and brand-focused marketing organization. Calibrating the type of marketing we do to the size of the business and the maturity of the brand in the markets we serve has been a moving target for us. As a product-driven company, we have traditionally focused on selling features and benefit stories of our innovative products. The majority of our competition in the climbing and skiing hard goods marketplace follows this model of product marketing.

The Black Diamond Equipment brand has been a successful differentiator for us, but our style of communicating the "Black Diamond difference" has been nuanced and subtle, to say the least. As we seek to become more meaningful to the lives of climbers, skiers, and outdoor athletes, telling a stronger product and brand story is the means to that end. As Black Diamond Equipment is one with climbing, skiing, and mountain sports, our challenge is to clearly articulate the simple truth of our brand: we make the best gear for climbing, skiing, and mountain sports because we are building this gear for ourselves, our friends, and our passionate and uncompromising community. Black Diamond Equipment is about great products we build for rigorous use during climbing and skiing *and* the connections we create between people who define their lives by these activities.

Central Brand Message

Our brand message centers on building trust in our expertise in and passion for mountain pursuits. Our experiences in the mountains push us to make the best gear possible for our international family of climbers and skiers. Engineering and product design are things that we are extremely passionate about, but what drives us is our dedication to these sports. This is the messaging we have woven through our materials over the years, and as we talk about doing a stronger job with brand marketing, we start to home in on some of the values that go deeper into what we do and how we do it.

Boldness, authenticity, and innovation define the Black Diamond Equipment brand platform, in general terms. These values will be stronger parameters for communicating our brand moving forward.

Conveying the Brand Message

Everything in our marketing, product, and sales approach must line up with the brand. It starts with our product and building a collection of products of consequence each season. Since BD is a living part of the sports we serve, there is a high degree of intuition in the products we build. We find that our values, wants, and needs line up with product design, which aligns with our sales group, along with the marketing group. Thus, developing a marketing mix pulls from the symbiosis we have within our organization and with the climbing and skiing markets in general.

With future product launches, we will roll out campaigns that are more unified and cohesively presented on our website that touch social media or traditional merchandising. By strengthening the BD brand, we will grow our group of users—both those that have been supporters and new customers.

Conveying the Company's Personal Connection

Our creative direction always emphasizes our intimate connection to those moments of consequence and inspiration that occur when you are doing these activities. We capture those shots and develop campaigns that convey intense intimacy with our sports because we know this is what resonates with our customers because we, ourselves, are our customers.

We also take public stands on issues of consequence to our customer base. Supporting local, regional, and national grassroots environmental groups that work to preserve the mountain, canyon, and climbing crag environs we rely on to feed our souls and allow our customers to recreate serves a dual purpose. In the *BD Journal*, our brand blog, we feature regular dispatches from BD employees adventuring in the wild, using our gear, and living the lifestyle that inspires us and our customers. In the *Journal*, we also feature informational and highly technical articles on how we test and develop our gear—also written by BD employees—as well as suggestions for gear maintenance and proper gear usage. These articles are among the most popular destinations on our website.

Marketing's Role in Development and Promotion

Marketing is intimately involved in the development of the brand, which is a combination of product, sales, and marketing efforts. I have the easy job of selling authentic stories that are not concocted from an esoteric abstract set of exercises. We are telling stories about real products for real activities; they are inextricably linked. We develop the most articulate way of explaining what goes on here on a daily basis at Black Diamond Equipment headquarters or any of the Black Diamond offices with the passionate employees we have. Our objective is to ensure we articulate what we do clearly and powerfully, without fabrication or artifice, mirroring our product design philosophy that says a product design is finished only when there is nothing more to take away.

Measuring the Brand Message's Impact

Over the past few years, especially as we have become more involved in online marketing, we have started recording the impressions generated by all of our marketing materials and programs. We then aggregate this information into what we call the marketing dashboard. We capture print advertising impressions and public relations impressions, as well as our media exposure and what is being generated by the events we attend. We look at online impressions through social media, including Facebook, Twitter, and YouTube, which provide a wide range of key performance indicators. We focus on bounce rate, new users, and conversion of specific programs. We also measure impressions generated by our visual merchandising POP programs that are moving forward.

We record all these metrics to be able to set goals annually. We then track those numbers monthly and review our performance, determine whether we need to re-direct our resources, and push forward if we see that we are hitting our goals. After years of just recording the data, we have now transitioned to driving the programs with this data.

Changes to Allocation of Resources

As previously mentioned, the efficient use of our resources is the principal reason we moved away from catalogs and completely out of print. The other programs we took a hard look at and are constantly reevaluating are our public relations (PR) efforts, along with our media planning. We continue to have a strong PR presence; therefore, we invest in these areas because it gains Black Diamond third-party accolades in terms of product awards. This third-party validation has a strongly positive impact at retailers with customer coming in looking for "award winners" from annual "gear guides."

In our media planning, we believe advertising in print and online media is still an efficient use of marketing resources. The massive amount of exposure a thoughtful and non-redundant media plan can deliver is hard to beat. However, the value of print media impressions is especially hard to measure. It is very difficult to determine how deeply customers are engaging with the print creative. Digital media performance is easier to track by straight-up click-though, but it is harder to deliver impactful digital creative with so much static in the digital media landscape.

The success of our grassroots program is the most difficult to measure of all our programs. There is great commonsense value to professional climbers and skiers using BD gear as they gain exposure through outdoor and even national media and films. But promotional venues for outdoor athletes are much more limited than other more mainstream individual, team, and Olympic sports. We also host or sponsor climbing, skiing, and mountain events, based around competitions, philanthropy, or community gatherings. Through both of these facets of our grassroots marketing efforts, we expose ourselves to far fewer customers than through the other programs, but these are very meaningful impressions and, when executed well, generate customer engagement that far exceeds what we can accomplish through other programs. Still, this is where our impressions analysis provides useful insights, as it allows us to determine how, relatively speaking, these events can be as impactful as possible, as well as how to provide a great Black Diamond experience to those who are most eager to engage with us.

At the end of the day, there is no ideal mix of marketing programs and no mathematical formula we have found to perfectly direct marketing resources. What is most important is a thoughtful business strategy that speaks to brand and product initiatives, alignment on what is truly driving the business where the products are sold today, and where it is all going in the future. The marketing program falls out of these parameters and should be an evolving mix of brand building, brand reinforcing, and speculative and foundational programs that drive customer demand in measurable ways that help report on performance and guide decision-making. And at the same time, a successful marketing program needs to create customer excitement and advocacy for the brand and the products in anecdotal and infectious ways that are not always quantifiable, but sometimes just feel right.

Opportunities for Athletic Sponsorship

We have both global and regional athlete teams populated by high-performance climbers and skiers who committed their lives to these sports and pursue them full-time. These athletes provide feedback on product prototypes and content for our marketing vehicles and represent BD in any media exposure they garner. Our global ambassadors receive cash, gear, and a travel stipend, as well.

We see tremendous value in our athletes appearing in movies and being profiled in global magazines like *National Geographic*, which presents our products to a much larger audience who may have never heard of BD. We believe it is a great honor to be a member of the BD athlete team. We are highly selective of our team members, and in addition to choosing athletes who inspire us with their accomplishments, we also prize good style, ethics, and humility in the ideal BD athlete. After all, these outstanding individuals represent Black Diamond and need to uphold the same high standards for integrity we aspire to live by and engineer into all of our products.

Addressing Negative Publicity

We have few problems with negative publicity. We work with people who share the same values and pursue their sports and their lives in great style. It is not just about being inspired or committed passionately to these activities, but it is also about doing these activities in a style that is respectful of others and the heritage of our sports. At the end of the day, we strive to maintain and grow a sense of optimism that people can treat each other well, respect the environment, and perform at the highest levels of sport.

Use of Social Media

We have been active in social media since 2008, maintaining a dynamic Facebook page, Twitter following, and YouTube and Vimeo channels. We have over 90,000 Facebook fans and have focused on growing that fan base over the past few years. The opportunity is direct communication with an enthusiastic audience that is significantly larger than most of the targeted vertical publications in which we advertise.

Our fans are extremely passionate about Black Diamond and sincerely want to engage with the brand. This captive audience presents a fantastic venue to deepen BD brand affinity among existing customers. We have done some apps on Facebook and some Facebook advertising. We continue to leverage Facebook as a targeted marketing resource and program. We are actively engaged in Twitter, as well, with more than 17,000 followers.

The more real-time and personal nature of these social media channels requires us to share another part of the BD personality that is less scripted and curated by granting access to the people of Black Diamond, along with our take on digital culture that falls just outside the limits of climbing and skiing. Based on the strength of the community's engagement with our social media efforts, we believe these BD customers are excited about having another way to interact with us.

We also recently started creating some contests on Instagram. While the last thing we need is another social media channel, we do believe the photo-sharing capabilities of Instagram are superior to anything else out there, integrate well with the other social media channels, and do what social media do best—make sharing our life experiences easy and quick. YouTube and Vimeo have been important for us in hosting videos and giving people other ways to experience or learn about our technology. We embed Vimeo players on our website and on other social media channels to provide optimized playback and syndicate our content through multiple channels, radically increasing broadcast power.

New Marketing Messages

Our upcoming messaging will focus more on BD brand values. We will do this through several significant product launches, brand-specific messaging, and new communication vehicles. We are building our apparel to line up with our brand values in the sports we are founded to serve: climbing and skiing. Apparel will generate greater interest in the Black Diamond brand, as well as grow the business as a whole, providing more exposure to the hard goods categories in the process. With apparel, we will expose both existing BD customers and an even broader group of consumers to the BD brand. While today, customers buy our hard goods—a set of Camalots or a set of skis—every couple of seasons, with apparel, customers will come back looking for new clothing, colors, and styles much more regularly.

Four years after we transitioned from print to digital marketing and a new website as our flagship marketing vehicle, we are redesigning the website again. The present site has reached the end of its useful life, as it will not scale to support the addition of apparel and new business initiatives. We will build a new website platform with more focus on brand messaging, deeper product technology information, and the latest best practices in user experience and features/functionality, and seek to provide our customers with a BD website experience that subscribes to our brand values emphasizing clean design, uncompromising functionality, and passion for the sports we serve, while seeking to match the positive experience every user has with BD gear.

Website Goals

By adding apparel into our product mix, we will now be selling to customers who shop with an increased expectation for merchandised product collections. Our global navigation and site architecture will need to undergo a significant transformation to best merchandise apparel, bring our categories and products closer to our customers, and make our whole range of gear easier to discover. We will incorporate customer reviews to help customers use community recommendations to guide their purchases. Responsive design principles will improve the rendering of our new website on whichever device the customer chooses to browse. We also plan to build in a new portal that allows for more dynamic customer engagement with the brand throughout the website.

As described above, we have made a significant investment in social media over the last few years and have effectively driven some great engagement offsite. We plan to bring more customer engagement on site through the redesign. We expect to do all this while improving customers' experiences browsing the site, learning which products are best for their intended uses, and then providing a great transactional experience, through either an online partner or the site directly.

Conclusion

The trick with marketing is to be able to build a program that is semi-modular and can effectively be broken apart and rebuilt to achieve the same success as the competitive technology and company landscape change. In this chapter we have looked at many specific tactics and programs I utilize at Black Diamond; yet what unite each of these are the brand values and core business strategy that drive the company forward. Through this lens, the programs themselves are evolving functions of the brand and business. And the marketing program as a whole is only as strong as a cross-functional team's ability to execute product and sales programs that are on the same page.

Marketing, at times, is a bit like juggling chainsaws. There are precision, timing, and danger if any one element gets seriously out of whack. My goal as marketing vice president is to constantly align the specific tactics—web, public relations, advertising, visual merchandising—and shift from product to brand marketing with the right allocation of skill sets within the departments. Even with an increased opportunity to assign metrics and perform analysis through marketing key performance indicators, marketing remains a discipline that combines data with intuition, much like the sports Black Diamond serves. You can have all the training in the world, good partnerships, and the right plan— but sometimes the mountains deal the cards. Maintaining an open mind, diligently working to stay abreast of changing technologies and new opportunities, as well as staying connected to your customers and knowing your brand, are all key tactics to continue climbing and build a marketing program that pulls its punches more than its weight.

Key Takeaways

- Ensure the brand message is made from real stories and is consistent throughout all areas of marketing. Well-defined brand values are the core of any marketing program.
- To maintain one's brand messaging, it is essential to partner with people who represent your company in a manner that is consistent with your company's values.
- When working within a sports market, it is crucial to partner with athletes on both a global and a grassroots level to express the importance of your company's brand and product.
- Maintaining a progressive and expansive view of all the marketing vehicles available is essential to growing a successful program. Be wary of sacred cows, as well as the marketing vehicle *du jour*.
- Brand development comes through the combined efforts of products, sales, and marketing groups; therefore, it is essential that they share a vision.

Adam Chamberlain, vice president of marketing for Black Diamond Equipment, grew up outside New York City, and the early years he spent exploring the Mianus River Gorge near his backyard ignited his lifelong passion for adventures in wild places. After graduating from Hamilton College in Clinton, New York, where he studied geology and creative writing, Mr. Chamberlain moved west to Bozeman, Montana, and Reno, Nevada, where he spent three years feeding his love for wild adventure and began a ten-year career with iconic outdoor clothing company Patagonia Inc. In 1998, he joined the US Peace Corps and worked as a natural resources volunteer in western Honduras. He returned to Ventura, California, to work for Patagonia Inc. in 2000 and spent the next six years working as content manager for Patagonia.com and then product marketing manager, ultimately directing product marketing initiatives for all business units.

Fulfilling his dreams of returning to the mountains, Mr. Chamberlain moved to Salt Lake City, Utah, in 2006 to work for climbing, skiing, and outdoor hardgoods manufacturer Black Diamond Equipment Ltd. as brand manager. To date, he has been charged with developing the company's internal marketing and creative horsepower into a true core competency, driving global branding and marketing initiatives, orchestrating an evolution of a print-centric to digitally focused marketing approach, and paving the way for the launch of Black Diamond Equipment's apparel collection in 2013. Black Diamond Equipment Ltd. went public in 2010, becoming Black Diamond Inc. (NASDAQ:BDE), and Mr. Chamberlain is responsible for the company's corporate marketing efforts.

Mr. Chamberlain and his wife, Kate, gave birth to their first child, Emerson Rose, on August 7, 2012.

Establishing Brand Leadership in the Fast-Evolving Mobile Market

Krishna Subramanian

Chief Marketing Officer

Velti

ASPATORE

Introduction

I am the chief marketing officer (CMO) of Velti, a marketing company committed to harnessing the power of mobile technology to transform communication, build connections, and drive value for brands and consumers alike. In this role, I lead the company's efforts to educate brands, mobile operators, and other marketers about the latest trends, strategies, and solutions within the fast-evolving mobile space. On a functional level, I am responsible for public relations, tradeshows and conferences, field marketing, product marketing and strategy, lead generation, and thought leadership. More fundamentally, I see my mission, like that of Velti itself, as being to advance the leading edge of mobile messaging to deliver better business results for brands and better experiences for consumers.

I joined Velti in 2010 through the acquisition of Mobclix, a mobile monetization platform I co-founded in 2008. As a small startup, Mobclix faced the challenge of being a relatively unknown company in a mobile advertising market that was only beginning to show its potential. The iPhone had just come out, and many marketers still thought of mobile in terms of flip phones and text messages—not the robust messaging channel it would soon become. This made it extremely difficult for us to raise awareness in the space, and to compete effectively against AdMob, at the time the leading mobile advertising platform. Unlike AdMob, Mobclix was not an ad network, although we did partner with many networks; spending our time explaining the nuances of this difference would risk losing our customers' attention. We knew that, for our voice to be heard, we had to deliver a message that was clear, sharply focused on business value, and extremely bold.

Toward the end of 2009, we launched a promotion based on a simple proposition: We challenged application developers to integrate Mobclix and AdMob side-by-side and compare the results. If Mobclix didn't generate more revenue than AdMob, we'd give them $10,000 in cash. The campaign was highly effective, generating considerable buzz in the market and convincing many developers to sign up with us. Most importantly, we established a clear message for our market: We help companies monetize their mobile applications through advertising—and we will put money on the line to prove it. That confidence helped establish Mobclix as a mobile partner that delivers results, and helped pave the way for our acquisition by Velti. Now, our combined organization continues to focus on helping companies achieve their objectives for mobile through proven expertise, solutions, and services.

As an engineer of marketing initiatives, I use data from Velti's ad exchanges and marketing campaigns to identify market trends from around the world and share this information with customers, developers, and the media. We show people the categories of apps they should focus on, how brands can best reach their target audiences, and what types of engagement are showing the greatest effectiveness, as well as creating the mobile platforms that people should be developing for. In this way, we provide not only solutions, but also thought leadership and industry innovation.

Differentiating Your Brand through Messaging

Over the past eight months, we have reinvented the Velti brand to better reflect the rapidly evolving space in which we operate. We have worked to position ourselves as both a leader in existing types of solutions and a key innovator introducing new ways to leverage the channel. As marketers increasingly focus on metrics and ROI, we have emphasized our focus on measurable results and business impact. Given the heated competition for talent within the mobile industry, we have also positioned our organization as the place to be for skilled and ambitious technologists, strategists, and marketers. A common thread runs through each of these themes: Velti drives innovation in mobile marketing. Every type of material we develop, from collateral and websites to product demos, reflects this vision.

Our marketing messaging is an important element of our brand development. For example, when we look at a data report from an ad exchange or mobile campaign, we examine it for insights that support our brand position: does the data support the value propositions for our solutions? Are there trends or impacts on business not seen elsewhere that we can highlight to showcase our unique vision and leadership? What avenues merit further exploration? How can we use this information to create a projected analysis of the future, and demonstrate how these trends will help position us for further growth and leadership?

Maintaining a Clear Message in a Changing Market

In recent years, Velti has operated three to four concurrent business lines; one of our key challenges has been to streamline our message and show a coherent vision even while the needs of our customers and the composition of our solutions evolve in tandem. One key deliverable for this effort is a national ad campaign that explains our mission.

While I do not anticipate eliminating any specific messages in the coming years, I do expect that our messages to various audiences will be continually refined and adjusted to reflect current reality. To provide unity and clarity across every audience we address, every message will reflect the core idea that almost anything can be mobile: any type of online activity, any type of marketing campaign, any type of retailing and commerce. Whatever companies hope to achieve on mobile, we are the only partner they need to get it done. We can help them identify changes in user behavior; for example, we can show that each laptop or desktop belongs to one user, and individuals are likely to own at least one, if not two, mobile devices. We can help them understand who their users are and which devices they use for various needs. We can help them advertise across the full range of devices on the market, and determine what types of messages are appropriate for different types of screens.

By helping people understand how to connect the dots across various platforms and devices while paying attention to the unique attributes of each, and providing the software they need to maximize the value of the channel, we will continue to strengthen our identity as the definitive partner for mobile marketing.

Measuring the Effectiveness of Marketing Messages

To reinforce the connection of the Velti brand to proven business impact, we emphasize the importance of measurement for our customers. How effective are the campaigns we run for them for increasing brand awareness? What kind of return on investment are they seeing? We also conduct studies to see how our customers are performing within their key markets.

Measurement is not just something we offer our customers; it is also a core part of our own business. We speak constantly with our customers about the results they are seeing with our products and solutions, and have them score our performance as a mobile marketing partners. We conduct surveys through a third-party analyst to see how effective our campaigns are and how we are perceived in the market. We also pay close attention to our market share relative to our competitors. Taken as a whole, this information helps us measure our ongoing improvement and makes sure our efforts stay closely rooted in reality.

Ultimately, we seek to regenerate the value of our marketing insight by leveraging our learning across every campaign we conduct, our own as well as those of our customers. Are we capturing and applying proven best practices? Are we tying our marketing campaigns together with the right message? These techniques have been highly effective for creating power-marketing programs for our brand as well as our customers.

Present and Future Challenges

The rapid growth of the mobile channel has brought challenges as well as opportunities. From a data perspective, it can be difficult to understand how all of today's mobile platforms blend together. User behavior, form factors, and device characteristics can vary significantly across platforms, complicating both mobile campaign development and efforts to analyze the performance of campaigns on a granular level. While there is no magic solution for this challenge, we make it our business to provide greater expertise in this area than the competition.

Infrastructure has also emerged as an issue; with so many new devices and apps entering the environment, carriers simply don't have the bandwidth or data capacity to keep up. This may lead to performance issues, rising costs, and other factors for marketers to deal with. One way we are dealing with this is to increase our focus on campaigns that are not entirely mobile-based, and to develop new offline strategies for connecting with consumers on the go. Again, as our customers face new challenges, Velti is always thinking two steps ahead to have the right solutions ready at the right time.

Conclusion: Core Elements of an Effective Marketing Message

As this discussion illustrates, the core elements of an effective marketing message are being able to understand who your audience is—in Velti's case, brands seeking greater clarity, measurability, and impact for leveraging the mobile channel for marketing; reaching them with a clear, compelling message to build awareness; and engaging with them continually by positioning yourself as a partner not just for today's needs, but also for the needs to come. In this way, you can build and nurture long-term customer relationships based on proven business value.

Key Takeaways

- In a fast-evolving market, it is essential to establish innovation as a core attribute of your brand, and to provide clear proof of your value proposition.
- Always allow your messaging strategy to evolve as the market evolves.
- Effective customer management is based on building long-term relationships. Focus on building and nurturing that relationship in order to create mutual benefits.
- The core elements of an effective marketing message include being able to understand who your audience is, how to reach them and build awareness, and how to continually engage with them.

Krishna Subramanian is the chief marketing officer of Velti and co-founder of Mobclix, a Velti company (acquired in 2010). Prior to founding Mobclix and joining Velti, Mr. Subramanian was co-founder and general manager of new business for BlueLithium, the world's largest behavioral targeted ad network that was acquired by Yahoo! for $300 million. Mr. Subramanian also launched MingleNow, the first online social network focused on offline places, events, and people. Prior to that, Mr. Subramanian was co-founder of Burrp!, a localized review and recommendation internet portal for metropolitan India (acquired by media conglomerate TV18). Mr. Subramanian is active in industry leadership, serving on the Board of the Mobile Marketing Association.

Mr. Subramanian's insights on mobile and interactive marketing and advertising have been sought after by major business media, and he's been interviewed by the New York Times, Wall Street Journal, Fox Business, USAToday, *and* Bloomberg *on numerous occasions.* Krishna *has written articles about the mobile marketing and advertising industry that have appeared in* MediaPost, TechCrunch, AdWeek, CIO, *and* Mashable, *among other prominent publications.*

He is a frequent speaker at conferences such as SXSW *Interactive,* OMMA *Mobile,* APPNATION, Digiday, AdTech, AlwaysOn, Commonwealth Club, *and* Communicasia.

The MedRisk Model: Successful Strategies to Reach Your Target Audience through Traditional and Unconventional Means

Ruth Estrich

Chief Strategy Officer

MedRisk

ASPATORE

Introduction

I am the chief strategy officer at MedRisk, a specialty managed care company primarily focused on the workers' compensation industry. In my position, I am responsible for network and new product development, vendor partnerships, and overseeing MedRisk's clinical and research subsidiary, Expert Clinical Benchmarks (ECB). My expertise includes the development and promotion of strategic solutions for US health care, insurance, and managed care industries.

For nearly twenty years, MedRisk has been the leader in the development and delivery of physical medicine management services to large insurance companies, third-party administrators, state funds, and self-insured employers. Traditionally, our sales and marketing initiatives targeted the corporate buyers and influencers at the executive level to sell program services. Our strategy evolved to rely on the client's management team to drive communications and mandate buying habits throughout all levels of their organization. However, the changing competitive landscape over the past five to eight years has resulted in more choices for physical medicine services at the desk level.

Major Marketing Communication Initiatives of the Past Five Years

To maintain MedRisk's position as an industry leader, in 2009, we launched a new initiative that involved repackaging our existing products, researching and developing new tools to support the desk-level buyer, deploying new platforms and infrastructure to support product enhancements and relationship building, and revising our go-to-market strategy.

This was a significant shift in MedRisk's previous marketing strategy, in which services and programs were packaged to appeal to corporate buyers and influencers. Traditionally, program emphasis was directed to technological innovation, clinical research and statistical analysis, and proof of concept and return on investment. However, for the product and services to appeal to the desk-level buyer, additional work was needed on the product and, ultimately, on the sales and communication strategies.

To that end, marketing worked with information technology (IT) and business analysts to research, develop, and deploy an online customer-centric portal. The portal allows users to submit a referral quickly and efficiently, find a provider anywhere in the United States, access active and closed referrals, track progress of scheduling and status updates at all times, copy and paste information into clients' claims systems, attach relevant medical documents, and access available reports, provider notes, prescriptions, and guidelines.

The portal also offers tools relevant to the desk-level buyer's job outside of physical medicine services, such as customized news feeds, charts, and free online continuing education webinars, to encourage continuous portal use.

New Support Infrastructure

MedRisk was one of the first in our industry to adopt cloud-computerized technology as part of our overall communication initiative and to support our new tools, product enhancements, and strategies. Implementing SalesForce.com into our overall communication initiatives has allowed us to facilitate new leads uploaded from trade shows, build on our client relationships, better manage our contact database, and improve our account management performance.

The new infrastructure has also helped us more efficiently manage and disseminate mass e-mailing campaigns, creating an easy and effective way to communicate with our clients, including adjusters, nurse case managers, and corporate executives.

Unifying Traditional and Unconventional Marketing Strategies

Right now, claims are piling up on the desks of workers' compensation adjusters and nurse case managers across the country. We think it is imperative that they know MedRisk is ready and willing to take that work off their desks. Using demand-generation efforts, the marketing team is committed to getting this message to potential desk-level customers. To build awareness and reach a wider audience, marketing is combining traditional strategies (trade shows, mail, advertising, field sales reps) with unconventional ones (social media, e-advertising, and mobile applications).

These efforts have successfully contributed to the company's goals of doubling referrals, increasing penetration, and "turning on" additional employers by reaching unaffiliated desk-level users.

With the launch of new, user-friendly services and the repositioning of products, marketing is in the process of executing a complete overhaul of corporate collateral, website content, and exhibit booth inventory. The objective is to continue promoting the MedRisk brand as the expert in physical medicine management, while highlighting our new, value-added services and ease of use.

Catering Communication to the Client

Our marketing initiatives are all designed to adapt to our clients' needs. This includes developing tools and promotional materials that incorporate important customer care facets, such as ease of use and excellent service.

In an age where most buyers (business-to-business [B2B] and consumer) obtain information via the web, MedRisk's homepage is the company's "storefront." Therefore, our web design must not only mimic the look and feel of our corporate collateral, but also clearly communicate the company's message and expertise.

For our executive clients, delivering this message involves distributing information they can use, such as industry trends reports, legislative updates, evidence-based practices, and information on how this information relates to the services MedRisk provides. We realize executives are bombarded with proposals and e-mails, so to best communicate our message, we deliver materials they consider valuable to their industry.

Communication tactics differ when dealing with desk-level users, busy professionals who value prompt service. They need someone they trust to take the work off their desks. Cost-savings is not a motivating factor with this audience. Adjusters want to know the nuts-and-bolts, while nurse case managers want regular, meaningful updates on the patient's progress.

The goal of our consumer marketing strategy is to communicate with desk-level users in a simple, no-nonsense way. We do this by maintaining our branding focus for this target audience, utilizing bright, bold colors and the familiar red "MedRisk man" icon. All marketing materials include language that is short and concise and answers the question: "What's in it for me?"

Collaboration Efforts of Marketing, IT, and Beyond

Over the course of two years, MedRisk has doubled the size of our marketing department, staffing it with experienced and talented professionals who are developing new strategies designed to generate new business and build our branding initiatives. In the midst of a recession, when other companies cut back on staffing to stay afloat, MedRisk hired additional talent.

To lead our desk-level customer initiatives, we added a consumer marketing manager who is responsible for developing, implementing, and managing the marketing strategies that target workers' compensation adjusters and nurse case managers. This individual's goal is to increase referrals by reaching the target audience through both traditional direct marketing and innovative outreach programs. This manager designs programs and tool kits to support the company's regional sales team and its initiatives, while clearly defining the company's message through consistent communication to desk-level users.

To boost our social media efforts, we also hired a media/communications specialist who has developed, executed, and maintained our social media platforms, which are designed to stimulate traffic, generate buzz, increase brand awareness, and grow business. This individual has launched and managed our Facebook page and coordinates our activities on LinkedIn. He also develops promotional materials for our public relations team, working to increase the company's visibility, influence, and interaction with its target market.

To improve the look of our promotional efforts, we hired an experienced in-house graphic design artist who brings a fresh look to our promotional pieces and is not afraid to think outside the box. This individual is a key player in our recent website redesign and has developed the layout and artwork for all of our marketing pieces.

In developing these online and social media programs, the marketing department worked closely with our IT department. This partnership was vital in designing programs, such as the adjuster portal, that fit our clients' needs. We also collaborated with our clinical staff to format and communicate our guidelines for practice and reference guides for treatment in an online design that is easily accessible to our audience.

MedRisk also partnered with SalesForce.com consultants to help implement our customer relationship management strategies for sales and account management and portal development. Additionally, marketing collaborated with ancillary industry experts to provide value-added products and services for our clients, such as continuing education, anatomical charts, and industry newsfeeds.

Another major hiring initiative occurred in 2009, when MedRisk expanded its sales force by hiring field representatives. These many individuals, who cover various regions across the country, bring our message "home" through face-to-face interaction with the adjusters, nurse case managers, and providers with whom MedRisk works daily.

Making Connections through Social Media and Mobile Technologies

MedRisk is heavily invested in using social media to promote our brand and connect with our customers. By communicating on our Facebook page and participating in industry groups on LinkedIn, we have developed social media platforms designed to facilitate conversations with our customers.

To strengthen our connections with our customers, our corporate initiatives in social media have primarily been directed at LinkedIn, where MedRisk executives often lend their expertise by participating in conversations with the most influential industry groups. Through these efforts, MedRisk enforces its position as a top authority in the workers' compensation field.

MedRisk's Facebook initiative involves a multi-level approach of customer-based and public-based promotion. Through our Facebook page, MedRisk has provided a home for our desk-level users by incorporating strategies designed to gauge their interest, such as funny workplace story contests, exclusive videos, and tools that can help them better perform their jobs.

Our content is also designed to reach the masses to help promote our brand to the public.

Aside from making connections to generate leads, MedRisk continually utilizes Facebook and LinkedIn to promote our value-added services. These include our free monthly continuing education webinars for nurse case managers and claims adjusters and our online portal for easy referral entry. Facebook has also provided a forum for promoting our presence in the field, such as conference coverage. By providing pre- and post-conference social media coverage through blogs, photos, and videos, we strengthen our brand awareness while providing a service to our clients who are unable to attend an event.

In addition to retaining connections and providing a networking forum for our clients, MedRisk uses social media to learn what our customers are saying about us. Monitoring social networks, blogs, forums, and tweets is one way MedRisk responds to critiques and compliments.

MedRisk is also building its application software to expedite the referral process for our customers. This includes a popular mobile app designed to help busy claims professionals manage their cases and their workloads on the go. By downloading the app on their iPhones or iPads, a workers' comp adjuster or nurse case manager can access the MedRisk program of physical therapists, occupational therapists, and chiropractors simply by using the mobile referral form.

And MedRisk utilizes the SalesForce.com enterprise cloud computing system to deliver mass e-mails to promote our presence at conferences, e-newsletters to update our clients on MedRisk news, and industry trend reports to bring our clients the latest evidence-based workers' compensation tools and information.

Key Differentiators Fuel Success

As a whole, our industry has been a late adapter to social media. According to a recent study by the Insurance Accounting & Systems Association (IASA), just 32 percent of insurance companies use social media for business networking. So when MedRisk launched our social media initiative in August 2011, we were among the first in our industry to fully embrace social media as a key strategy. As a company that mostly works in business-to-business dealings, our goal was to develop our Facebook page as a means to promote our brand to the masses and develop closer ties to our target audience, which includes insurance claims adjusters and nurse case managers, and providers, such as physical therapists, occupational therapists, and chiropractors.

In a matter of months, we have developed a huge following and have created a strong social community. Our content reaches hundreds of thousands of viewers each week, significantly outperforming the social media efforts of our direct competitors. To help build our fan base, we incorporated a successful monthly contest called "The Cube," in which fans can enter a funny or unusual workplace story for a chance to win a $100 gift card. To further invite participation from our followers, we allow them to vote on the entries and choose the winner.

Another key component of our Facebook content is our coverage of national conferences, which features blogs, photos, and exclusive videos that only our fans can access and enjoy. This includes our popular video feature, "Got a Minute." These man-on-the-street videos feature workers' comp experts lending their expertise to a certain topic of interest. By providing social media content that is useful, entertaining, and thought-provoking, MedRisk has expanded our promotional reach to one that goes well beyond that of our competitors.

Conclusion

The last five years have proved a challenging and exciting period of growth for MedRisk. As new competitors have entered the market, MedRisk has stayed on top of our field by doing what we do best—adapting to our clients' needs by developing tools and services to enhance their productivity. In the midst of one of the worst economic downturns in US history, MedRisk not only retained its valuable staff members, but also hired additional talented professionals to help expand our program and launch new marketing initiatives.

As a pioneer in our industry, MedRisk has not rested on its laurels, but has stayed ever committed to maintaining our position as the leading force in physical rehabilitation management, by incorporating new media strategies into our sales and marketing protocols. To strengthen the continuum of service through our insurance and health care partners, MedRisk has developed new marketing initiatives and products designed to empower desk-level users to do their jobs efficiently and effectively.

Key Takeaways

- Stay on the forefront of technology. Use new media to connect with and expand your client base. Provide your clients with new ways to interact with your products.

- Develop clever campaigns designed to attract your entire audience. There are no one-size-fits-all strategies when communicating with your clients. Develop specific initiatives that incorporate the needs of those at the desk and corporate levels.

- Combine traditional and unconventional marketing strategies to maximize the audience your message will reach.

- Recognize that your webpage is often your first point of contact with potential clients. Be sure to make a good first impression with your online "storefront," so that it reflects your business accurately.

- Use social media to expand your brand awareness and involve your target audience.

A dynamic industry expert with more than thirty years' experience in managed care, group health, and property and casualty insurance, Ruth Estrich, chief strategy officer of MedRisk, is a leading voice in the workers' compensation industry. As part of the executive management team at MedRisk, she is responsible for network and new product development and account management, and she oversees MedRisk's clinical and research subsidiary, Expert Clinical Benchmarks (ECB).

As the president of the Insurance Accounting & Systems Association (IASA), Ms. Estrich leads one of the insurance industry's largest and most well-represented trade associations. A popular industry speaker, she has addressed such conventions as IASA's Annual Conference, National Workers' Compensation Insurance ExecuSummit, the Institute for International Research, the National Workers' Compensation Symposium, the Financial Risk Management Forum, the National Workers' Compensation and Disability Conference, and the Risk Management Society (RIMS).

ASPATORE